The Night Cleaner

To the Tractor

The Night Cleaner

Florence Aubenas

———

Translated by Andrew Brown

polity

First published in French as *Le quai de Ouistreham* © Éditions de l'Olivier, 2010

This English edition © Polity Press, 2011

Ouvrage publié avec le concours du Ministère français chargé de la Culture – Centre national du livre

Published with the assistance of the French Ministry of Culture – National Centre for the Book

Polity Press
65 Bridge Street
Cambridge CB2 1UR, UK

Polity Press
350 Main Street
Malden, MA 02148, USA

ISBN-13: 978-0-7456-5199-6

A catalogue record for this book is available from the British Library.

Typeset in 11 on 14 pt Goudy
by Servis Filmsetting Ltd, Stockport, Cheshire
Printed and bound in the U.S. by Edwards Brothers, Inc.

For further information on Polity, visit our website: www.politybooks.com

Contents

Preface

It was the recession. Remember? It happened a very long time ago, ages and ages ago, last year.

The recession. People talked about nothing else, but they didn't really know what to say about it, or how to gauge it. They didn't even know where to look. Everything seemed to suggest that the world was collapsing. And yet, all around us, things still seemed in their places, apparently unaffected.

I'm a journalist: I felt I was facing a reality which I couldn't explain, because I couldn't get my head round it. Words themselves failed me. Even the word 'recession' seemed to me, all of a sudden, as devalued as the shares in the stock market.

I decided to head off to a French city where I have no attachments, to look for work, anonymously. It's a simple idea. Many other journalists have put it into practice before me, with great success: a white American man became black, a blond German became a Turk, a young Frenchman joined the ranks of the homeless, a middle-class woman swelled the numbers of the poor, and there must be others I have forgotten. But I allowed myself to be carried along by the situation. I didn't know what would become of me, and that was what interested me.

Caen seemed the ideal city: neither too far north nor too far south, neither too big nor too small. And it's not too far from Paris, which I thought might be useful. I came home only a couple of times, for a flying visit: I had too much going on in Caen. I rented a furnished room.

I preserved my identity, my name, and my ID, but I signed on as out-of-work with just a baccalaureate in my pocket. I claimed I'd just separated from a man I'd lived with for some twenty years; he'd provided for all my needs, which explained why I couldn't show that I'd done any work outside the house all that time.

I became blond. I kept my glasses on all the time. I didn't receive any allowance.

With more or less certainty, more or less insistence, a few people paused when they heard my name: a social service advisor, a recruiter in a call centre, the boss of a cleaning business. I denied that I was a journalist: I just had the same name, I claimed. Things went no further. Just once, a young woman in a temping agency rumbled me. She was following the rule book. I asked her to keep my secret, and she did so. The vast majority of the men and women I encountered didn't ask me any questions.

I'd decided to stop once my quest was accomplished, in other words the day I got a permanent contract. This book relates this quest, which lasted almost six months, from February to July 2009. The names of people and businesses have been deliberately changed.

In Caen, I kept my furnished room. I went back there this winter, to write this book.

Paris, January 2010

I

Scraping the Barrel

In Cabourg, the house of Monsieur and Madame Museau is located in one of the new districts situated away from the beaches and the sea wall, far from the crowded streets and the five-star hotels, sheltered from all the hustle and bustle and the pretty touristy bits. Here, in this unremarkable, comfortable suburb, those who live in Cabourg all year round can flourish.

It's February, and the sky is dark and oppressive. On this particular day, Monsieur and Madame Museau are waiting for a housekeeper – she's supposed to be arriving at 2.02 p.m., on the bus from Caen. It hasn't been easy, deciding to employ someone for this kind of job, and they have thought long and hard about where to interview the applicant. The living room seemed too formal, the office too cramped, the dining room too intimate, and the kitchen too disrespectful. Finally, they've gone for the conservatory, a draughty room that they don't usually open except in summer.

Today, Monsieur and Madame Museau's conservatory is the only window lit up on the façade of the house overlooking this tranquil street. As a result, they can be seen from a little way away, through the big bay windows, as if on the bright stage of some theatre. He is standing up, wearing his jacket, unable to keep still, roaming round the table. Sometimes he stops to jot something down on a notepad lying on the table in front of him. His wife gets up and comes back with a pullover. She is wearing make-up, and has done her hair with some care. They pull up a chair opposite them. He looks at his watch. She does, too. Monsieur Museau glances outside, just as I am turning onto the white-gravelled path between the garage and the hedge. He turns to his wife, no doubt to tell her, but she is already on her feet. The door is open even before I've had time to ring the bell.

'Are you the housekeeper?'

This is my first job interview since I started looking for work, in Caen, in Basse-Normandie.

In the conservatory, Madame Museau motions me to the empty chair.

Monsieur Museau had given me advance warning on the phone. 'We're both retired. Actually, if you know what I mean, Madame Museau's always been a home body.' He'll be doing the interviewing, he declares, simply because he's not used to it happening any other way. 'I know all about hiring people, I've managed up to five hundred employees, I ran various businesses. You know Bernard Tapie,* the businessman? I've had the same career.'

---

* A well-known businessman, TV personality, and former Socialist government minister who spent six months in jail for corruption.

With his ravaged face, he imperiously weighs me up. He talks about his health, two heart operations – he's quite willing to give me the details. The conclusion comes with a brutality that he savours. 'With everything I've gone through, I'm not going to be around for long.'

I feel it's only right to protest, but Madame Museau interrupts me straightaway. 'Oh yes, with everything he's gone through, he's not going to be around for long.'

'At the moment, we're still doing a lot. Madame Museau does the ironing. She looks after the housework. She does the cooking. She does everything. But, well, I'm saying *at the moment*. We'll be doing less and less. And when I'm not here, Madame Museau will be left.'

'Perhaps I'll be the first to go . . .' remarks Madame Museau, like a threat.

'Anyway, just remember that Madame Museau herself would never have hired you. She'd just never have thought of it. I'm the one that's looking ahead. I organize things. I take the decisions.'

'You talk too much.'

Her handsome features barely move. She must have put up with a lot from him, never able to get her own back.

Monsieur Museau goes on, as if he hasn't heard. 'We've decided to take someone one while we're still okay. I've drawn up a list of the good points of the job we're offering. First, you'll have your lodgings. We'll put you up in the room of one of our grandchildren. There's a single bed.' He looks me up and down. 'That'll be fine, you're the right size, you'll fit. And anyway, things can change perhaps, later on.'

He laughs to himself, scrutinizing me one more time.

Then he resumes. 'We'll clear out all the junk from the room. Do you have a lot of stuff? I guess not. We'll put some furniture in, we've got all the necessary in the house. Too much, actually. Second good point: you'll have your board. Madame Museau does the shopping in the supermarket, right next door. You can go with her. She buys things, you can tell her, "That's what I like." She'll put it in the basket. Do you see what I'm saying? It's informal. Sometimes Madame Museau will tell you, "I'm tired," and you'll go and do the shopping by yourself. She also likes going to Carrefour. It's further away, but it's bigger. It means she gets to see people. Madame Museau does the cooking, but you can give her a hand. You can lay the table. You'll tidy up after, you'll take the plates away, but you'll eat with us. How shall I put it . . .? I don't want to have someone in the kitchen and then us in the dining room. No, never – I really don't like that.' He hesitates. 'I'm a bit of an old so-and-so, aren't I? My wife tells me: "You have a cold, hard way of talking." Well, it happens. It's only to be expected. I've had up to five hundred people working under me. Did I mention that? Yes? And for Bernard Tapie too – I told you? I was in the building industry.'

'You're talking about yourself as usual,' concludes Madame Museau.

'Anyway, let's get back to your *life résumé*, as I've decided to call it,' says Monsieur Museau, as if he hasn't heard a thing.

He picks up the page of notes in front of him, and asks me for my date of birth. He jots down: '48 years old, sign of the zodiac: Aquarius.'

He goes on: 'You did the literary *bac*, right? What did your father do? Civil servant? Yes, but where? There are all kinds of civil servants. Then you say you were a cleaner. You didn't need to work. You've just separated, that's why you need to start looking for another job. You don't have children. But what about him – any children? He hadn't married you, of course? On what date exactly did you separate?'

On the sheet of paper, Monsieur Museau writes: 'Separated five months ago.'

He continues: 'Are you still seeing him? Have you remained on good terms?'

He notes down: 'Good terms.'

Monsieur Museau reads it all through, and ponders. 'Basically, he used you: you did everything, and then, when he didn't need you any more, it was goodbye. That's about it, right? And he must have found another woman by now.' His analysis satisfies him. He carries on, as if thinking to himself: 'She's younger, I imagine, perhaps much younger. Well, I'm going to leave you with Madame Museau now, she'll show you upstairs, your room. We've got four children, two are in Paris, a daughter and a son. They've got good jobs. What does Christophe do? I've forgotten. A telephone company, I think. My daughter is very active. She's a Museau. Christophe is a Resthout, like my wife – you can see what she's like? – but Christophe is all right. All the children are all right. The youngest lives with us. Her name's Nicole, like the woman who comes to do the ironing, but we call our daughter Nicky. She's an estate agent in Lisieux, she's thirty-seven. When I'm poorly, she gives me a hand. She won't leave. Too scared. We try to kick her out. It'll be too late in ten years' time, you know. Let me tell you a story so you'll understand the situation. Madame Museau had a friend, a long time ago. What was her name, that friend of yours?'

Madame Museau doesn't like having this story told. She looks sulky, and tosses her pretty head.

Monsieur Museau seems particularly glad to be embarrassing her. 'You called her Fifi, right? You won't say? Fine by me. Anyway, Fifi lived with her mother, she looked after her, she did everything. Her other brothers and sisters had left. When they came to visit, their mother would take them to one side. She told them, "You know, Fifi's trying to poison me. She puts things in the food she cooks me. She's going to inherit everything, you won't get her out of here."'

'When people get old, they don't know what they're saying,' Madame Museau breaks in. 'Anyway, you're telling the story all wrong. Nobody can follow it. You mix things up to suit yourself.'

Monsieur Museau flaps his hand to shut her up. 'We don't want there to be any difference between our children. I absolutely want Nicky to have her own apartment in Lisieux. She'll leave once we've got a housekeeper. There. I've had my say.'

Madame Museau escorts me through the house. She has

always polished the broad red tiles – very shiny – in the hall-way herself, and made sure that everything is strictly tidied away. 'Now I don't feel like doing it at all. I ask myself, why bother?' Without her husband around, she cheers up, and even permits herself a smile. She opens the door of 'Monsieur Museau's office', on the ground floor. He lives here – everything suggests as much, the crumpled sheets on the bed, the folders scattered around, the computer permanently blinking on standby.

Upstairs, we quickly walk through Nicky's room, where, in an overwhelming stench of tobacco smoke, there are piles of chocolate bars, tottering heaps of magazines, and clothes screwed up into bundles. Madame Museau is in a hurry to show me her own territory, behind a white door at the end of the corridor.

'How much would you like to be paid?' Monsieur Museau has popped up behind us, calculator at the ready. Madame Museau gasps in surprise. He is delighted. 'Scared her! Scared her! Did you see how scared she was? Shall we say 1,000 euros? Think about it. On top of that, there are the perks I mentioned, you get board and lodgings. It's your call. I can even go a bit higher.'

He's just taken the car out of the garage. 'That'll do, you've seen enough. Madame Museau will show you her room next time. Come with me. I've decided I'm going to drive you back to Caen.' The engine's already running.

The countryside speeds past, flat and quiet. The weather's turned almost nice.

'I've driven so much in my life that sometimes I didn't even know why I was on this road or that one. I drove straight ahead, thinking: where on earth am I going? I wanted to succeed.' All of a sudden, Monsieur Museau adopts a confidential tone. 'You know, I was in the same situation as you, to some extent. I left home with someone for a while. I left Madame Museau and the children. I came back when I fell ill, but we still meet that other woman. We invite her to our home in Cabourg. She has dinner with us at our table, she sometimes stays for a few days. You'll see her. Madame Museau badmouths me when we have company, but never when we're alone together. She doesn't say anything in front of me. She's reserved. She's used to this situation.' He thinks for a while. 'Right now, Madame Museau must be sitting on her bed, wondering whether I'm not overstepping the line with you.' He smiles, his eyes half-closed, imagining his wife.

'Anyway, you'll be taking Madame Museau out. One of our children died young, you can go and visit the grave, it takes a whole day, it's a change of scene. You know, she never left home. When we had the twin girls – one is very Museau, by the way, and the other's a real Resthout – , she got a maid straightaway, a Polish girl. We called her Piroshka. You can go and see her too, she lives in Louviers. That's another idea for a day out you can have together.'

This schedule has cheered Monsieur Museau up considerably. He puts the radio on. Switches it off. Puts it on again. Sings then speaks. 'I'm homeless – my property's in the name of my children. I've built it all up for them, I love them all,

Museaus, Resthouts, whatever. But I'm still the boss, you know. I tell them what I'm doing. Usually, they don't quarrel. They tell me, "You know what's what, and in any case, you never listen when we talk to you. You do what suits you."' He laughs to himself. 'It's true. I'm the boss. I do what I want.'

He's missed the exit, at the roundabout into Caen, and now he's furious. 'We natter away and look what happens. You forget everything when you're old. Get out here, you can walk the rest of the way, it's much better than getting the bus, you've been lucky.'

I'd never intended to work at Monsieur and Madame Museau's. I don't want to go into service for individual people, or live in the intimacy of their household – this is the one stipulation I made in my quest for employment. Apart from that, I'm ready to accept any kind of a job. It merely turned out that it was Monsieur and Madame Museau who replied to my request the first. I'd been looking for a job for a fortnight – an eternity, it seemed to me. The days dragged on forever, shapeless, irritating: I was being forced to wait, and none of my attempts seemed likely to succeed. So I didn't resist. I wanted to see what a job interview was like, and to feel that I'd finally got something going for me.

I'd already been round the temping agencies in Caen. They're all clustered round a few streets near the railway station, and they're almost all built on the same model: an empty room with a desk. In one of them – the first, I think, though

I now mix them all up in my memory – , I triumphantly announce, 'I'll take anything.'

'Everyone will take anything in this place,' says the boy behind the computer.

I ask him what's available right now.

'Nothing.'

On the other hand, he sees all sorts of people coming by, including his colleagues from the temping agency next door, where they've started laying people off. He says his turn will come, maybe. He looks out at the street through the window; his round face remains motionless, reflecting neither hope nor fear. And he concludes, a little solemnly: 'It's the recession.' From the church tower of Saint-Michel, which towers over the housing block, a few chimes ring out into the peaceful afternoon.

One after another, the agencies refuse to take my details. It's like being treated by a nurse in a ward for palliative treatment – gently but firmly. The questions come raining down, always the same. Do I have any experience in temping? No. Do I at least have any recent experience, of any kind, in Caen? No, and no. 'So you can't be classified as one of the really, really reliable people, the Zero Risks,' another young man in another agency points out. 'These days, the Zero Risks are the only ones employers want for temping. There's a special file for that, even for twenty-four-hour temporary workers at the hamburger factory.'

Behind me, people I've bumped into in the previous branches are waiting. I'll be seeing them again in the next ones, no doubt. Some just push the door open and shout from the threshold, without even loosening their scarves, surrounded by little clouds of condensation, 'Anything for me today?' It's a 'no' everywhere on this particular day.

I stubbornly defend my chances of getting a job that's advertised in the window: 'Salesperson to give advice on animals (living and lifeless) in pet shop department of superstore just outside Caen.' The agency employee is almost shocked. 'This is an offer for a very good job indeed – really top drawer. You don't fit it at all.'

I ask, 'Why not?'

He seems more sympathetic now. 'But you're a bit . . .' I can see that he's trying to find a word that, without being hurtful, will still be realistic. He's found it, and gives me a big smile. 'You're more like, scraping the barrel, Madam.' It's said without malice, good-naturedly.

The man working in a laundry watches me leave the agency. 'You don't want to hang around there, Madam. Everyone can see you're lost.' I suddenly see how naïve I'm being. With more resolve than experience, I've come to Caen to look for a job, convinced that I'll find one, since I'm ready to do anything. I was fully prepared for working conditions to be tough, but the idea that I wouldn't be offered anything at all was the only possibility I'd not envisaged.

I give the temping agency opposite another go. It's a young girl this time, barely out of school. She shakes her head. 'You won't get anywhere. It's too hard. You need someone to give you a leg up.' She continues, 'If you've got friends in the right places, I can try and take you on. Do you know people here?' I don't know anybody in Caen. I say, 'Bye then, I'll come back.'

The young girl smiles. 'No, I've told you already. No point in coming back. Thank you, Madam.'

2

A Rush Job

It was Pôle Emploi agency which suggested that I become a cleaner. It all happened very quickly, without my altogether realizing it. I'd officially signed on at the beginning of March 2009, without any fixed ideas. I'd be given several job offers, naturally, I'd have time to weigh them all up before reaching a decision. At least, that's how I imagined it.

At my very first interview, after ten minutes or so, an advisor told me, in a sensible tone of voice, 'The best solution as regards your personalized plan for gaining access to employment is to turn to a particular speciality: cleaner.' Just as I heard myself reply 'Yes', the advisor's hand was already shaking mine, nice and firmly, as she saw me to the door. There we go: sorted.

Around 10.45 a.m. on the day I sign on, there are about fifteen of us waiting in one of the eight Pôle Emploi sites in Caen. It's busy, but not noisy; there's a careworn, dense, almost tangible tranquillity that amplifies every sound. Everything seems designed to create a sort of blank discomfort, where nothing invites you to settle down, or even to linger any longer than the time absolutely necessary for the formalities. The room is a big lobby which acts simultaneously as a reception desk, a waiting room, and a telephone cabin for people to pursue their quest. You can also consult the job offers on computers. These functions are not separated by any partitions, and everyone is standing, behind counters as tall as a man, so that the people, the agency's advisors included, seem to be floating around the draughty space, between the drab-coloured walls. These areas don't have a chair or a desk, either. Everyone seems to be avoiding the only place where it would be possible to sit, a few chairs soldered down by metal bars, placed in front of a screen. A Pôle Emploi film on an endless loop repeats like a nursery rhyme: 'You have rights, but also duties. You can be removed from the register.'

On some days, nothing happens, and the queue grows shorter smoothly. On other occasions, someone will suddenly explode. This morning, it's the woman just in front of me. And yet she starts calmly enough. 'I was called in about a job as a canteen attendant. It was a contract for a few hours a day in a town near Caen. They told me, "You're just right, you'll be first choice for the post." Then, nothing. Two months later, I get a phone call telling me that in the end they took someone else instead of me.' Her voice rises a tone. 'So the person tells me on the phone that this other person – the one who was taken instead of me, not the one phoning me – isn't any good and the first person – the one phoning me – is asking me to come in again because, in the end, it's me that's going to get the job.' At the counter, the advisor tells her that

she's not in the right place. 'Here we don't manage jobs as
such. We just put employers in contact with job-seekers.'

People around are starting to grouse. They mutter that
this woman's making them waste time. Someone else loses
her cool. 'Nobody's got the slightest idea what she's talking
about.' A young man protests, 'If we all start trying to get
things off our chests, where's it going to end?'

The woman couldn't care less. 'But I saw the advert here
– so you're responsible! Let me tell you what's really happened. When this other person eventually let them down in
the town council, they said to themselves: we just need to
get back in touch with the second choice, the old girl. Me.' I
look at the naked face of the 'old girl', her hair done in a tight
bun, her brand tracksuit ironed with a neat fold, her hand
clutching a shiny black bag. She must be much younger than
me.

The employee from Pôle Emploi again tells the 'old girl'
that she needs to take it up with the town council in question. Nothing seems capable of stopping her. 'Finally, they
took a third person.' She heaves a sigh. And continues,
louder: 'What do *they* have that I don't?' Now she's shouting:
'I – need – to – work!'

The whole agency has come to a stop. The photocopier is
emitting flashes of white lightning into the empty air and, at
the far side of the room, faces have popped out, one by one,
above their computers. The only sound that can be heard is
the trilling of mobiles, which nobody answers, and the voice
of the film intoning: 'You have rights, but also duties. You can

be removed from the register.' Hypnotized, we all watch the shiny black handbag that the woman keeps whirling around in short bursts, as if it were the ball in a tennis match.

An advisor suddenly emerges from a corridor. In a strong, calm voice, he draws her to one side, away from the queue. The advisor has only one thought in his mind: what if she's armed? He often talks about this possibility, with his colleagues. They tell each other that, one day, there's eventually going to be a real drama, someone's going to come into the agency, smash their faces in or take a pot shot at them. There'll be one dead, or perhaps several. At times like this, an image always springs to his mind, that of an American high school he's seen on television after a pupil committed a massacre. There were the same walls painted in faded colours, but they were spattered with blood; the same chairs with ends that were too pointy, but they'd been knocked over every which way; the same scrupulously clean floors, but they were strewn with dead bodies. The TV newscaster had spoken of 'carnage'.

The advisor looks at 'the old girl'. Her hair is a little dishevelled, she has red blotches on her face and the bewildered appearance of people who've just been woken up. He says, mechanically, 'We'll look at your file together, Madam.' He remembers saying the same words the day before to a young girl and a dog, both of them equally furious.

The other day, somewhere in the east of the country, other colleagues were apparently kidnapped by a client. There are more and more incidents in agencies, and a special dossier, called the 'security register', has been opened to keep tabs on them all.

This is all going to end badly, the advisor is sure of that. He finds it difficult to fix his attention on this woman's papers, as if he just can't grasp her situation. Now she's talking to him in a dull, mechanical voice: 'I'll give you my ID number and my personal code, Sir.'

'Let's have a little look at that together, shall we? Do you have the name of the agency you're signed up with, and the name of your referee?'

'Of course, I always come with all my documents, Sir.'

Further away, the queue gets smaller, and muffled noises emerge from it. One fellow has started making calls from the phones put there for job-seekers to use. His side of the conversation can be heard. 'Hello, it's me, have you got my documents ready for a work placement?' Then, 'You can trust me, I swear it, I've stopped messing about. Thirty years . . .' There's a silence. Then: 'No, not thirty years inside, you moron. It was my thirtieth birthday. I meant that I'm not a kid any longer.'

I am seen in a room at the end of the corridor, where my ID documents are photocopied. Various pages are filled. The main part of the discussion focuses on the best way of getting to the first steering interview in a different office at the other end of Caen. There, I will be 'given guidance in my job-hunting quest'. I need to show up there that very afternoon, or, at the latest, the morning after. The procedure insists that the time between the two formalities should not exceed twenty-four hours. This is the new *modus operandi* of the administration. Everything has to happen at the right place and the right time, so as not to swell the statistics. The employee utters a discreet laugh. 'The administration needs to show how efficient it is.' She points a finger at me. 'And you too, eh?'

A bus drops me off at 2.10 p.m., the same day. I'm on time. It's in the Mémorial district, this time. In the middle of a monumental esplanade, planted with flags, I lose myself among the tourists visiting the Peace Memorial Museum.

The agency is further up. It looks like a shed. Inside, it's divided into little cubicles, each with a desk and two chairs. A set of thin partitions separates them from one another, like screens, without going right up to the ceiling. The interviews take place here, amid the hum of conversations and people coming and going.

An advisor watches me come over. In the course of an afternoon, she sees a dozen newly registered clients queuing up, all of whom need to be assessed before they can be given guidance. There didn't used to be any limits to the length of these interviews. Orders from above started to restrict them to half an hour, and then twenty minutes. Between colleagues, the phrase used is 'a rush job': everyone is reluctant to do it like that, but the directives are clear: 'You're not social workers any more – those days are over. We need figures. Start calling the job-seeker a "client".' It's official: this is the word from on high.

For a long time, the staff responsible for job-seekers *did* mainly comprise social workers. But these days, recruitment essentially targets salespeople. 'Get it into your head that it's a new profession. The familiar old system is dead and gone,' the managers keep saying.

This atmosphere has been prevalent for a long time, but a gust of panic swept through the agencies a few months ago. It has not abated. Suddenly, during winter 2008, we were officially declared to be in a recession. The radio talked about it morning, noon, and night. Every day, 3,000 more unemployed signed on with the agencies, and in a few weeks the administration found itself struggling under a mountain of 70,000 unexamined files. Such a thing had never been seen before. In Paris, management was terror-stricken at the idea that social security might not be paid in time for the party season – people would be demonstrating out in the streets, and a Red Christmas would sweep the country, a whirlwind of decorations and rebellion. Everyone was put on notice to get through as many files as possible. They managed just in time, but since then, things have never been quite the same.

Only the aims and objectives have not varied: they need to do better, from one assessment to the next, whatever the economic situation. For 2009, it's a matter of making 3% more job offers than in 2008. The number of adverts also needs to increase by 13%. But only on the Internet: this stops employers visiting the agency, and prevents the telephone lines from getting jammed. Increasing productivity: that's the priority.

It's quite impossible. What's going to happen? The employee sighs. She's just getting up to greet me, but another woman has already stepped forward and motioned me to a chair in her cubicle. She has a good eye for detecting the right client, the one she's going to place quickly, the one who won't end up ticking the fateful box 'long-term unemployment'. If there are too many of these in an agency, they reach saturation level and collective bonuses fall.

Anyway, the right client has a few qualifications, a bit of experience, a nice little car. This is what they call 'profiling'.

'Do you have a vehicle?'

'No.'

She stares at me. Off to a bad start. A car is the employers' first criterion, even for activities that don't require one. It means they can place you, it proves that you have at least enough to fill a tankful of petrol, that you're not scared to go out of town, that you can cover a reasonable area.

'Single woman? Over forty-five? No particular training? No recent pay slip?'

In my advisor's eyes, all the red lights start flashing. I've just entered the Statistical High Risk zone.

She tries one last question. 'Any children to look after?'

When I reply 'no', I see her breathe for the first time.

In the cubicle next door, a man is asking in a muffled voice to be given some training as an electrician. He says he is used to his habits, to a certain standard of living. 'I've already ticked the boxes for restaurants and so on. We could sell the house – the children have left home. But I need a placement.'

My advisor asks me what I want to do.

'Anything.'

I thought this would reassure her as to my fate, but she seems to find it unexceptional. She scans my résumé, which stops at the baccalaureate, followed by the mention of a few little jobs as a shop assistant or waitress. After that, nothing.

'What have you been doing for the last twenty years?'

I repeat the story I told Monsieur and Madame Museau, the same one I'm going to tell everyone, my alibi: I met a man who kept me, then ditched me. Now I need to work again. I've revised the script several times over in my head; it seemed pretty clever, I even invented a profession for this man in case the questions became more searching. He worked in a garage, in the Paris region. I'm just starting to spin out the whole tale when my advisor politely interrupts.

'Just like everyone, basically.'

Next door, the man is now explaining that he used to be a policeman. He repeats it several times over, each time uttering the syllables in a different tone. A voice tells him, 'Listen, Sir. Training courses are expensive, we have priority lists for registration. You're not a high priority. You need to understand that.' A silence. 'After all, you're fifty-nine.' The next applicant is already standing ready, his coat on.

I'm not entitled to any allowance. My advisor stares at me reflectively, looking as if she were sincerely concerned about me.

'Do you want to start a new life? How about working with maintenance staff? The cleaning professions are the future, but you need to make your mind up now. The market is being structured, it'll soon be full. They're setting up courses to train cleaning professionals, with a specialized *bac*, perhaps even postgraduate studies. In one or two years, businesses will only take on qualified housewives. It'll be too late for people like you, without any qualifications. You need to launch out right now, otherwise you won't stand a chance.'

In the next cubicle, the new client sits down. He says straight out that he's perfectly happy to earn less than the minimum wage. The advisor protests. 'Is this the latest fashion or something? You're the third person to tell me that today. You know it's against the law?'

'But if it's me that suggests it, it's possible, isn't it?'

The advisor doesn't follow this up. She says, 'I can see that you used to be a marketing advisor. What about being a sales rep? Though there are sometimes three trips to Paris and back per week.'

'Yes, I can do that.'

From my side of the partition, I tell my advisor that I'm quite happy to go into maintenance. I'm entitled to do a one-day course on 'The Cleaning Professions', to attend a 'Résumé' workshop, and to receive 'assistance with my job-seeking' for three years, from a private consultancy, all as a Statistical High Risk. A piece of paper indicates that my 'main specialities and conditions of work are the routine cleaning of premises and work services, picking up waste paper, cleaning furniture and accessories (ash trays, waste-paper baskets, etc.), management and follow-up of jobs at various sites'. I sign on the dotted line.

I haven't even been here for a quarter of an hour. Later, several of the people I talk to will ask me if I was forced to accept this job. Not at all. On this particular day, I even felt a huge sense of gratitude towards my advisor.

The furnished room I rent was being lived in by a student in the first year of her law degree; her parents live in a village on the coast. She gives me the keys with a sigh of relief that positively transfigures her. At last she is returning home to live with them, working on the railways, like her father.

The room occupies half of an apartment that the owners split up to rent it out. You need to push the desk to open the window, and fold up the sofa-bed to get to the sink. Outside, you can see a small yard, other apartments, the sky. Everyone tells me I've been really lucky to find this apartment, especially right in the middle of town. On entire pages of adverts offering accommodation, for days on end, I saw only one that said 'Will take a worker'.

In the evening, I phone the Museaus to tell them I won't be taking their job as a housekeeper. It's Madame who picks up the phone. Before I even have time to speak, she shouts, 'Wait, I'll get my husband. Monsieur Museau, it's her – come on!' Then, 'He's coming, he's coming. Oh come on, get a move on, Monsieur Museau!' Finally, 'Here he is, I'll put the loudspeaker on.' I stammer out an excuse, another job that I've found in Caen. She says, 'I understand,' and hangs up straightaway.

Tomorrow I'm going to Bayeux, and this prospect puts

me in a good mood. They've organized a jobs forum in the Novotel there, 'with fifty businesses', as the leaflet specifies. It's less than twenty miles away from Caen. There are going to be a huge number of job adverts and offers, apparently.

3

A Lunch

Early in the morning, a train full of schoolgirls takes a quarter of an hour to cross the countryside from Caen to Bayeux, making the kind of hubbub associated with dormitories and boarding schools. The ticket inspector pushes open the door to the compartment and steps hesitantly in. The laughter and jokes uttered by the girls submerge him like a wave. He stops, blushing, and turns round.

At Bayeux, there's a salty wind blowing, damp with rain, glazing the restored little streets, the cobbles, the English-style pubs where, even in broad daylight, the reddish-brown light of a neon sign glimmers. Statues covered by velvety moss keep a vague guard over churches and houses. Sometimes, at the corner of a street, the cathedral suddenly looms up, and its shadow quickly swallows everything else.

I ask my way to the Novotel, where the jobs fair is being held. I'm going completely the wrong way. I have to walk down past small squares and gates, through which I catch a glimpse of verdant gardens and town houses, of the kind you don't usually imagine finding here. Small workshops with a patina of age are followed by antiques shops and museums, as tranquil and motionless as the waters of a pond. After the Second World War, Bayeux was nicknamed 'la Miraculée', being the only city to have emerged from the bombings intact. Without noticing, I've moved from one district to another. Now I'm walking back down perfectly straight streets with recent pointy-roofed houses built along them. Then the blocks become higher and higher, and the cars are being driven faster and faster. By the time you get to the motorway feeder road, in the industrial estate, you're there.

At the entry into the Novotel, Bayeux's entire complement of job-seekers is jostling for place, with everyone brandishing the letters instructing them where to turn up. As soon as you go into the entrance hall, you see job adverts pinned up on big notice-boards, highlighted in every colour, as in a shop window.

One group is already gathering around the most alluring prospect, the prize display of the whole jobs fair: a position as a mason, with a permanent contract, for 10 euros per hour.

'Refuse collector – that's well-paid too,' someone remarks.

'How much?' asks a young man with fiery ginger hair.

'The main thing is you only work four days a week.'

'How much are you paid for the training?'

'There ain't no training, you idiot. What training do you need? All you have to do is chuck plastic bags into a bin lorry.'

'There *is* some training. There's gotta be some. You get

trained for everything. I did some training to be a swing repairer. And the training was paid.'

'These gingers! Bloody idiots the lot of 'em.'

'I'm not ginger!'

The other ads are all offering jobs at the minimum wage – 8.71 euros per hour, gross – often just for short periods. Every post bristles with restrictions, and is hedged around with imperatives: they all appear inaccessible. Take the job as a receptionist, a six-month contract at the minimum wage: you need a specialized baccalaureate in receptionist skills, you must speak English to bilingual level, hold a driving licence and a car to go with it, and have an address in Bayeux.

Inside the fair, stands with the logos of different enterprises are giving information to job-seekers. I'm eager to take my first steps in my new profession. There's only one cleaning company, I rush over to it, clutching my sheet of info from Pôle Emploi.

The young woman who receives me has applied a long line of mascara, giving her the eyes of Cleopatra. She asks, 'What's the first thing you do when you arrive?'

'When I arrive where?'

'You know, Madam – when you take up your job at a particular place,' replies Cleopatra wearily.

I'm fully aware that this is a trick question. Actually, it will always be the same question – but this is my first time. I don't know.

'You need to open the windows to let the air in,' says Cleopatra tartly.

She promises to call, but I never hear from her.

Most companies reserved their places here before the recession hit. They've still turned up, but mainly just to put in an appearance, not to offer any jobs. Under the pennon of an estate agent, someone on work experience is cheerfully handing out cups of coffee. 'The sector's screwed. There are going to be some second-hand BMWs on the market.'

Most of the visitors have congregated in front of three stands: Frial, a local frozen foods factory, and two hypermarkets. In front of one of the latter, there are about thirty of us waiting. Forms are handed out, and we fill them in, waiting our turn. The biros are passed from hand to hand, we all copy each other's answers.

'What are you putting for the question "What job do you see yourself doing in ten years' time?"'

'Me, I really stick my neck out. I write: working at a check-out desk. Can you imagine my family, the face they'll pull if I go home tonight and tell 'em, "In ten years' time I'll be working at a check-out desk"?'

It's my turn with the recruiter. It's ten in the morning, he seems tetchy. He tells me, 'We've got a job as a shopfitter vacant.'

'That's just what I'm after!'

'Why?'

I flail around for an answer. 'I love everything to do with fixtures and fittings, I think I'd have loads of ideas.'

'Shopfitter, in our books, actually means sticking up notices on the shop ceiling. You'll be in a pod, like on a big wheel, 25

feet up, with some screwdrivers. Do you suffer from vertigo?'
I start to flail around again, but in the other direction. 'I
love climbing, physical work, funfairs. I've always found the
big wheel so romantic!'

He stubbornly continues to gaze down at his knees, which
he can fit behind the tiny desk only with the greatest difficulty. His pen settles on his sheet of paper, ready to write
something, hesitates, and then stops without noting anything
down. I can't catch his eye.

He adds, 'You need to be there at six in the morning'.

'Great, that suits me, I'm an early bird.'

The pen is completely immobile, suspended high above
the paper. He says they'll contact me, perhaps; he clearly
emphasizes the word 'perhaps'. Finally he stares at me and
frowns. 'In any case, if you don't reply straight away, they'll
telephone someone else. They don't have time to chase up
applicants.' He waves at the pile of résumés on his desk,
dozens and dozens of filled-in questionnaires. The point of
his pen indicates the exit. I realise my time's up.

Someone from an employment agency is offering 'speed
job interviews' in the tone of voice of a fairground barker.
'You go head to head with an employer and you've got a
minute to sell yourself. Roll up!' Three or four kids, always
the same, pick up the prize each time. The employment agent
soothes the losers. 'Don't worry, it's all virtual, like a game on
TV. There's not really a job at the end of it.'

As I approach a notice 'The land army seeks recruits' (right
next to 'The police force seeks recruits' and 'The navy seeks

recruits'), someone comes up to me, booming, 'How many résumés have you submitted this morning?'

'Six.'

He says, 'Congrats, you win! I've submitted five.' He holds out his hand. 'Philippe. Mind if I see your résumé?' We exchange our life stories and each of us reads the other's résumé, standing up in the aisle, in the midst of people jostling past us. A woman in military uniform comes over and asks us to move on. 'What about the air force? They not recruiting? I'd like to be a squadron leader,' says Philippe.

'I don't find that funny, Sir. We're here to provide jobs – a national priority.'

We go back to the entrance hall, where the throng around the advert for the 'full-time mason' has swelled even more. Philippe re-reads my résumé, as if looking for something in it. Then he finds it. 'But you live in Caen, you're not from Bayeux! What are you going to do about lunch? Come round to my place!' His hair is combed backwards, a bit long at the neck, a mixture of blond and grey, and he's wearing a signet ring with a wolf's head.

Today, he's going to cook me his favourite meal – rillettes, pasta, and ham. It's his winter speciality. In the summer, he goes out on the balcony and grills sausages. He also does veal Orloff, whatever the season, but he's never sure it'll work. He prefers not to run the risk. He winks. 'You'll try it someday, I hope?' Philippe lives near Bayeux, on the edge of another bypass. By the time we've reached the front of his block of flats, we're on friendly terms. We start by paying a visit to the new dustbin area, with its very special sorting system. 'The block has a very good reputation, as you'll see!' says Philippe.

His flat is amazingly spacious, at least three rooms, very simply furnished with a table, chairs, a sofa. It appears more bare than empty, with its uncurtained windows, its smooth walls and floors. In all the rooms, the red and green standby lights of an impressive array of electronic gadgets blink on and off. I don't know where to sit, or even to put my bag down.

'Have you just moved in?' I ask him.

'No, I've just got divorced.'

Philippe puts on a Johnny Hallyday CD, and switches on the TV and the computer in the living room.

He refuses to let me help him lay the table. I can recognize my place from the display of containers arranged in a semi-circle around my plate: ketchup, mayonnaise, three types of mustard, saffron sauce, Roquefort sauce, rouille sauce, pesto. A napkin has been placed in the middle, with – for no particular reason – the words: 'Happy birthday, darling!'

Philippe has been looking for work for six months. Conversation on this subject is rapidly disposed of. 'I've been left hanging about before, but I've always got something in the end. What about you – first time you've been unemployed? You'll see, after the second time, you don't feel so scared. It stops feeling like a fatal condition – you get by. So long as you're ready to start all over again from scratch.' He explains that he likes every kind of job, but not every kind of woman. Philippe, it turns out, is looking for a woman, and he's readier to talk at much greater length about this than about work. For both women and work, he's got a trump card, he says. 'Look at me. You've got to guess what it is.' I scrutinize him. I have no idea, but I don't dare to tell him so. He laughs, a real hearty guffaw. 'Are you shy? Or can you really not see? It's my eye, the left one. It's practically dead. For employers, they get extra points for a handicapped worker: it's in their interest to take me on because they'll get tax deductions that way.' I ask, 'And what about women, why's your eye such a trump card there?'

'It makes me look deep and enigmatic, don't you think? No?' He seems genuinely surprised when I don't react more. 'Well, some of them have already told me so.'

We take another helping of pasta and rillettes.

He continues: 'I'd like my wife to be just like you, with the same face, the same kind of clothes, the same way of eating. Exactly the same'. He laughs. 'You don't happen to have a twin sister, do you?'

I immediately invent a husband I live with in Caen.

'So where are you going to tell your husband you had lunch today?'

'I'll tell him I had lunch with you. He doesn't have any reason to get worried.'

Philippe seems almost hurt. 'What do you mean, no reason to get worried? A man always has a reason to get worried!' Annick, Philippe's first wife, left him for the man who came to install their satellite dish. He was there to wire the whole block for cable, so they'd had time to see each other for days.

She went off, taking the motorbike and both of their helmets with her, including the one with little multicoloured lights which they used to take it in turns to wear. Philippe had his children with Francine, the next one. He'll show me the photos in a minute. She became an alcoholic, but it took him a while to realize. Ever since, he's stopped putting wine out for women when he invites them back. It's a kind of test.

In addition to his eye, Philippe has other advantages that he's quick to list. For example, he can take someone round the museums of Bayeux on a Sunday. In the evenings, he sometimes plays cards with friends, belote mainly, and tarot too, but he feels quite ready to pack it all in for the sake of a woman, especially at the start, when you're still head over heels. In any case, there are women who like card games – belote, tarot, all sorts. His friend Patrice was married for a long time to a blonde woman, she even taught them how to play poker. They've since divorced, Philippe can't remember why.

When I tell him I need to go, he offers to come with me to the station, by bus of course. 'Don't go back to the job centre, someone will probably start chatting you up. There are plenty of guys that only go there for that, you need to be careful.' He's folded my résumé and slipped it into a frame on the TV, replacing a postcard on which two arched dolphins are announcing in a cloud, 'Everything's going swimmingly in Deauville!' My telephone number is on it, he points to it and says, 'I'll call you.' Then he laughs, with his good-natured laugh. 'You can tell your husband that, too!'

In Caen, it's pouring down. It's 3.30 p.m., it's already growing dark, the cars are splashing through puddles with their
headlights on. I push open the door of the second-hand dealer
next door to my place. He's looking for someone to help
cleaning out attics. He tells me I'm not the right person, but
doesn't explain why. When I persist, he just goes on working
as if I wasn't there.

My 'work placement in cleaning' starts tomorrow morning.
When I registered for it, the other day, at Pôle Emploi, an
advisor told me, 'Above all, put on some clean clothes. And
no high heels or revealing shorts.'

4

The Beast

In the entrance hall of the vocational training centre, each new arrival is met with nothing in the way of friendliness or sympathy. One after the other, we come in and gather round the coffee machine, standing in a circle as if it were a stove. Nobody dreams of taking off their coat, even less of having a cup of coffee. We move in slow-motion, kicking our heels, shuffling around, taking sideways glances. Soon there are a dozen of us, all ages, including two men, all waiting for the start of the 'work placement in cleaning'.

It's half past nine, one hour has already gone by when two sturdy young women decide to launch into a conversation.

'My cat can't stand my boyfriend.'

'My cat gets on fine with my boyfriend, it's my dog who doesn't like him. The other day, when I went to the vet's, I couldn't resist: I bought two tame rats.'

'I've got some goldfish, too. I think they've paired off, but I'm not sure.'

'Fish just don't do it for me. Not in the slightest. I've got three budgies in the same cage.'

'I couldn't care less about this placement. I don't want to be struck off by Pôle Emploi. That's the only reason.'

Someone asks me if there's an exam at the end of the day, but nobody knows. One of the two men is almost sure that some of us are going to be failed, 'come what may'. It's the same everywhere, there's just not room for everyone. The girl with the three budgies shrugs. She has the healthy complexion of people who live out of doors. 'I haven't turned up empty-handed, I've got a qualification: a vocational training certificate in looking after the elderly.'

A tremor of anxiety runs through the rest of the group.

The other girl carries on. 'We used to have a pit bull, but we had to give it away. When I did the shopping, he cost me more per week to feed than me and my boyfriend. We couldn't manage. We'd already borrowed from the family so's we could carry on paying the rent. The flat's too dear, but we don't want to let go of it – we'll never get another one, now I'm unemployed.'

'My cat's been traumatized. My ex-boyfriend used to knock it about, so it's a bit disturbed.'

Still we wait. Sometimes, one of us goes out into the street to gaze down its long, quiet curve, bordered by a cemetery and two florists'. One of the young women runs off to have a look at the price of the pots of chrysanthemums and then comes back.

Finally, the two instructors open the door: a man and a woman. We've automatically all stood up straight, even the two sturdy young women. The instructors seem borne in by a gust of fresh air. They're excited, they laugh, they stride along, they make a noise. They are young and seem nice. They have a whiff of the outside world, full of busy people and days chock-full of activity. They've made a silly mistake: they've come from Rennes and they forgot to check how much petrol they had. They apologize and giggle again. This has put us all in a good mood.

They're going to explain to us what the work of maintenance staff consists in, and they warn us, 'It's got nothing to do with what you think it has.'

Now we've settled down in a basement room that's arranged like a lecture hall. Some slides show us maintenance staff in various places. The male instructor has gone off to the service station. The female instructor gives us a commentary on the images.

'The main quality consists in working quickly. The cleaning company sells hours'-worth of cleaning to the different companies that ask for it. You generally come in outside the working hours of the other employees, in other words very early, or very late. If you get a toehold, you'll manage to get a few hours mornings in one office, a few hours evenings in another, and sometimes contracts in fits and starts in between. You need to want these if you're going to get on. The employers demand skills.' Then she asks, 'What does that mean – skills?'

She waits for a while, and eventually gives the answer herself. 'It means knowing things, knowing what to do and how to do it.'

The woman next to me leans over. 'I'm glad I didn't say anything.'

Other slides pass before our eyes.

'By the way, to work in hospitals, you need to be able to read and write. It's almost compulsory, since there are often lists of instructions to consult and carry out.

'In a shopping centre, you might feel ashamed about being seen in overalls by people you know doing their shopping. You need to be straight about your job. Often, the places get dirty straightaway: you've just cleaned them, and somebody throws up in exactly the same place. You feel you're not getting any gratitude for your job.

'In the bus, you need to get used to cleaning one window out of every two. It's a pain – you'd like to wash all the panes the same, that's the way you were brought up, it's just the way. But it's not possible, you don't have time, the employers calculate the working hours to the last second. The windows are the hardest job, but the most in demand. A window cleaner can always find work. There are international competitions for window cleaners.'

Next, we watch a film. A man in overalls, accompanied by a vacuum cleaner, comes into a room where another man, this one in a suit, is sitting at a desk. The employee in overalls says, 'Hello.'

'I'm showing you these images because it doesn't come easily to everyone to say hello,' explains the female instructor. One of the two men on the course, who has introduced himself as Maurice, asks if he can speak. He says, 'You should also knock before entering. They pointed this out to me when I worked for a company for a couple of days'. The instructor continues, 'In a business, you'll meet a lot of people who won't say hello to you, or won't reply. This is no reason to hang your head and sulk. You need to grin and bear it. Cleaning work is a state of mind, too. Once, in a bank, when the office had closed, one girl decided to do the cleaning in her underclothes because she was too hot. You need to watch out. There are CCTVs in some places.'

Karine shrugs. She says out loud: 'Obviously.' Karine is just twenty-five years old, and I don't think I'm going to hurt anybody's feelings if I say that she is far and away the prettiest of us all. She's also the best student on the course. Her hair is cut in a bob, it's very, very black, and she slowly blinks to show her eyelids, which she's covered with a very, very thick blue turquoise.

Karine gazes at the slides like all the rest of us, but don't be fooled. She's already worked in cleaning for over a year, she's followed a two-month full-time course, and she's even had what is usually called a modicum of success.

Everyone turns round to her and asks her to carry on. She plays a bit hard to get. But not too much. She speaks with a self-assured voice, imbued with a certain boldness, which stands out against the awkwardness and mistrust that none of us really manages to shake off.

Karine had initially taken a training certificate in sales, as she felt a vocation for this. She still has a bitter, vague memory of that period, as if it had been a time of humiliation in which the only question her bosses asked her concerned the size of her own trousers. A marriage, a child, two children, unemployment and more unemployment. Karine was pointed in the direction of cleaning. She signed up for some classes given by the ex-housekeeper of a big four-star hotel, a powerful woman, who set written tests. Karine had a hard time of it before emerging among the best in her class, which none of us would have doubted.

'And what happened then?' asks the woman next to me. A cleaning firm spotted her and gave her a job straightaway. The place she worked was one of the nicest in Caen: Karine had her little trolley, like in the brochures, with various cleaning products, two buckets, and microfibre cleaning cloths in every colour, including pink for the toilets. She feels in a position to say that she's cleaned everywhere that can be cleaned: Caen prison, the Zénith concert hall, a fishmonger's, schools, hotels. Karine was always available, even in the evenings, at weekends, for overtime, on holidays. She was punctual, she stayed in a good mood even when the hours she worked overtime were actually never paid. She returned home in the middle of the night, walking along the expressway when her husband needed the car, and she never complained.

Karine gazes at us and lowers her turquoise eyelids. Suddenly her voice becomes husky and harsh in a way nobody would have anticipated: 'If you don't do all of that, you're done for. You've had it. You cease to exist. If you scratch the bosses' backs, they'll scratch yours. You have to stay on the bottom rung if you're going to make it.'

The female instructor, as if to echo her words, says, 'You don't make any demands to begin with. You need to prove yourselves first, learn to become accepted.'

Karine has become a much sought-after cleaner, piling up every hour imaginable, morning, evening, and in the middle. She's even imposed her own rules for window cleaning. 'Normally you have to do it American-style, moving the squeegee round and round. But I told them, "I'm French, I do it the French way, horizontally." Nobody dared to tell me off.'

At that moment, sitting there in the room, we all know that Karine's story is quickly moving towards a tragic end. We are gagging to hear it. Karine continues in her muted voice.

One of her contracts was for work in a very chic business, one of those fashionable firms everyone fights to get into, even if only to do the cleaning. The boss lady had her dog and this dog used to do its business everywhere. Karine cleaned up once, twice, three times, on her knees on the fitted carpet, rubbing away behind the dog's arse, her head buzzing with all the accumulated exhaustion. One day, she told the boss, 'You need to take your dog out. I'm fed up with it.' The boss was sorting through her handbag. Without looking round, she said, 'But that's what you're being paid for, isn't it? To clean up shit.'

'Shit, maybe, but not your dog's shit. I've got a dog too, twice as big as yours, but better housetrained.'

Her boss spun round and walked towards her. Unable to

say what went through her head just then, and unable to regret it much, Karine saw her lift her own hand and bring it down on the boss's face. She adds: 'It wasn't a heavy slap.'

Karine's employer asked her what she preferred: to give in her notice, or to be sacked. She was advised to continue with her studies. She refused. 'I'm twenty-five, I've got two kids. It's too late. I'm not going back to school.' She doesn't know what she's going to do: temping, perhaps.

On the screen, we look at a new slide without really seeing it. In it, an employee is piling cut branches into a lorry. 'Shall we meet up again after lunch?' says the female instructor.

I ask, 'Anyone like to come with me to the baker's?' We set off with two ladies and walk up to the shopping centre in the Grâce de Dieu district, which isn't very far. For everyone in Caen, the names 'Grâce de Dieu' and 'La Guérinière' – the neighbouring district – arouse the same reaction, in particular among those seeking council housing: 'Anywhere, but not there.'

In the middle of the blocks of council flats, opposite the tram stop, a bar sells lottery tickets, tobacco, and stationery; next to it, there's a greengrocer's, a mini-market, and an iron-monger's that also sells equipment for mint tea. And yet the place enjoys a certain renown. People come to visit it from far and wide, from the countryside all around and even from the city centre. It occupies an entire corner of the block, indicated by the signs that run down the façade. This is the chemist's. The price of the medicines here, it is said, is lower than you'll find anywhere else.

We go, more modestly, into the baker's. One of the ladies doesn't buy anything, the other counts out her change for a pain au chocolat. They say they're not hungry. We sit on a bench, it's a bit chilly but, between two blocks of buildings, a triumphant sunbeam shines right into our faces, sending spangles of dazzling dust flying into the air.

I say, 'It's really nice on this bench.' The lady with the pain au chocolat looks at me in astonishment. 'I'm really bored sitting here with you lot. At this time of day there's *Mind Your Step* on TF1,* and then the news. Sometimes I switch over, but not very often. It would be so nice to be watching TV. I really miss it! It makes me ill.' If she dared, she'd go up to one of the flats in the block in front of us, ring one of the doorbells and say, 'Mind if I watch your TV?' People wouldn't be scared, they'd see she's not dangerous, she'd huddle up on the sofa. How happy she would be.

She gazes quizzically at the sun, the buildings, the crumbs of pain au chocolat scattered all around her. Then she says again, 'How boring it is.' Her husband's very into the Internet. He plays games, roulette and casino. They've practically stopped quarrelling since they started subscribing. The other lady isn't really listening. She keeps getting up and sitting down again, or rather sits up and then flops down again on the bench, as if being pulled by a violent force. This

* In the original, *Faites attention à la marche*, a TV quiz.

morning, she didn't take the children to school. Nor yesterday. No energy. She swears she'll go tomorrow. She knows
she won't.

In the afternoon, we have a practical session. The young
male instructor has slipped on an immaculate white coat that
makes him look like the doctors in the toothpaste ads. He's
going to tell us how to use a mop. He waves a squeegee, at
the end of which there's a cloth soaked in a cleaning prod-
uct 'which attracts and soaks up dust, thanks to a chemical
procedure too difficult to explain'. But the really big thing is
the 'shampoolux', an electric machine for shampooing the
floors: it sprinkles them with water and soap as it scrubs them.
He warns us, 'They call the shampoolux the Beast, because
everyone's scared of it. You have to be able to control it,
otherwise – disaster! It can smash into the furniture. You
need to be really careful.' Everyone in the audience utters a
big 'aaahhh' when he starts the motor. One of the two men,
Maurice, has suddenly stood up to seize his chair by its back
and use it as a shield, as if the Beast had spotted him and was
getting ready to charge him.

The instructor calms us down. He sets the shampoolux
going. In his hands, the Beast suddenly looks just like a
harmless vacuum cleaner. He makes it do pirouettes and
shampoo tiny corners, stops it just an inch away from
Maurice (who pulls a panic-stricken face), then forces it
to set off in reverse gear, swaying along jerkily, roaring like
a wild beast under the trainer's whip. When he unplugs

the Beast, we all applaud, spontaneously, feeling a kind of relieved tenderness. We've had a scare, then a good laugh, and now we're all getting ready to go our separate ways home when the male instructor tells us: 'Now it's your turn. You're each going to have a go in turn, and I'll give you a score for your course report.'

Panic breaks out: real panic. One woman is almost sick. Another dashes off to lock herself in the toilets. One or two try to sidle out. A hubbub breaks out, making everything inaudible except for a few piercing phrases: 'No way, I'll never get the hang of it,' or 'I can't do it in front of everyone else, the others will all stare at me, it'll make me curl up and die.' There are cries and sighs, and eyes start to water. People start fanning themselves, including the two sturdy girls, who look as if they're being led to the scaffold.

One of them keeps saying, 'Right, that's it, I'm screwed, I'm really screwed.' The men gravely pace up and down.

'Who's going to go first?' asks the instructor as if he hadn't noticed a thing. He sighs that it's always the same when the tests start: nobody will volunteer. Eventually, someone steps forward. 'I've got my driving licence. Do you think that'll help?'

A heavy silence weighs on the whole scene, except for Karine, who giggles: 'The first time I did it, I ran over the instructor.' One of us is sent to stand by the mains, and told to pull the plug if the Beast turns out to be uncontrollable. Everyone manages, more or less, to master it for two or three yards, as far as a little wall. That's the whole point: either you manage to make the Beast do a U-turn so you can head off in the other direction, or else you crash into the scenery.

When it's my turn I manage, with difficulty, to get by – just. 'Handling the mop and the shampoolux: not quite up to the expected level,' says my report. But it adds: 'Shows willing.'

5

The Maid

It was at this time, when I was finding my feet in Caen, that I got to know Victoria. I even remember the date, 19 March 2009, when the unions all called us out for a big national rally against the recession. There couldn't have been a better day for meeting Victoria.

I remember it as if I were there now. In Caen, the demonstration is scheduled to set off from the place Saint-Pierre at 10 a.m. Long before this time, a dense crowd has covered the whole square, and people continue to flock there, like a human buffer zone extending from the area in front of the church to the walls of the chateau; they flood into every available space, into the entrances of buildings, the tourist information office, and even the yard in the police station. It's as if the whole town has emptied out onto the cobbled streets. The local residents have even seen Suzy, their neighbour from the rue Victor-Lépine, a chambermaid from a hotel opposite the railway station who was recently widowed. Her husband worked for customs, he died suddenly last year, dropped dead in the bathroom. He might not have liked her going on a demo – who knows? As for Suzy, at all events, everyone's been saying it's the first demonstration she's been on, she took her place under a random banner, right at the start, then gravely followed it for three hours until the march dispersed, and she looked exactly the same all the time, as if she'd been escorting a religious procession.

The sales girls in the clothes shop beg their boss to let them join the demo, they've seen the check-out women from the big store and the girls from the fish shop. They want to be part of it all, too, please. And the boss finally agrees, with a smile like Father Christmas: go on then, it's a special day, it's been a long time since we saw this kind of thing. The boss has seen plenty of big workers' demonstrations going past – it's a ritual in Caen – and he prides himself on being able to recognize the type of march it is, to distinguish between the annoying and the scary ones, those that make the customers grouse and those where you need to draw the shutters down. This time, stare as he will, he can't make it out at all.

The sales girls rush to the door without bothering to pick up their coats. They can't even get out onto the pavement. The demonstrators form such a compact mass that it blocks the entrance to the shop, as hard and motionless as a great wall. The sales girls laugh their heads off. 'The one time we want to go – what a laugh!' One of them says her husband must be somewhere in the crowd. He was curious to join the demo this morning. He kept moaning, 'It's always the same lot that go on strike, and never me.' Then he griped about the flat that they can't afford; about the football that he'll have to watch on TV because the tickets to see it at the ground are too dear these days; about life itself, which is getting worse every day. And off he went to join the demo, his lips pouring out so many complaints that you can see him still chuntering away to himself in the street.

I've been told about an association for the unemployed. I keep an eye open for it, and come across a few people who belong to it without openly ranging themselves under its banner. Stéphane and his friend must be the only ones, or almost the only ones, to have pinned onto their work over-alls a prominent badge, 'Action Against Unemployment'. Stéphane hasn't turned thirty yet. He's just been laid off at the Trucks company, like 700 other part-timers. He gives a tight-lipped smile and says, 'I'm lucky. The boys were nice: they didn't chuck me out there and then. I was able to finish my contract.' At Trucks, one of the bosses announced the other day that the order book was showing a drop of two-thirds. The assembly lines are rolling less and less at weekends, the boys are laid off for half the month. On the shop floor, it's all anyone is talking about: people *being let go of*, as they put it. Nobody knows what's going to happen, who's going to be affected, or how many. Sometimes, people say that it'd be better to leave of your own free will, rather than wait to be thrown on the scrap-heap. They say, 'One way or another, let's draw a line under it. It's driving us crazy.'

Trucks used to be called Saviem, then RVI, one of the biggest local firms, with 6,000 assembly workers for Renault lorries, near Blainville, along the river Orne, on the old naval construction site. One day, at the end of the sixties, the police all drew up next to the hospital in Caen to wait for the demonstrating strikers marching in that direction. The result: twenty seriously wounded. Two days later, the Saviem workers came back, and the ensuing riot lasted all night. In the seventies, the days of union action against unemployment started off with tear gas and ended up with smashed windows, whole streets of them, right in the city centre. There was also the NMS, the Normandy Metallurgical Society, nicknamed the 'workers' fortress', one of Caen's industrial legends with its 7,000 staunch men at the blast furnaces who spread their anger across the whole town and generally ended their demonstrations by lashing out with bludgeons. These days, people still say it's a miracle nobody was ever killed. And what about Jaeger? And Citroën? And the Radiotechnique firm? And Blaupunkt, which changed its name three times before becoming Valeo? There were more than 20,000 jobs across eight big factories strung out in a circle round Caen, all pointed to as an example of how France was able to combine its fields of potatoes with its coke furnaces, and how the country had picked itself up after the war and was decentralizing its industries amid marshland, ducks, and bombed-out buildings.

These days, here and there, a few traces survive of the fragmentary assembly shops forever marginalized by corporate restructuring. In under a century, an industry was built up and then completely wiped out. Moulinex was the last big one to close down, in 2001, after negotiations in Paris, marches, and coverage in all the French media.

Today, 19 March 2009, the demonstration is still growing, but there's no anger in it, no real slogans, as if its only claim to attention lay in its sheer mass. The crowd is huge, absolutely enormous, and has even ended up by swallowing the very people who called it out into the streets – the unions. You can sometimes make out a chant, a flag, floating over people's heads, like a lifebuoy more than a rallying sign. The procession no longer seems to be borne along by certainties or grievances, but merely crisscrossed by questions, which fly from one group to the next: 'How many of us are there? What are we going to do? How long's it going to last? Where are we going?'

At the end of the rue Saint-Jean, on the bridge across the Orne, everyone stops to take photos of each other. A couple of pensioners are amazed. 'But there's only pensioners at this demo!'

'Mum, Dad, that'll do!' says the tall thirty-something walking with them. He himself is holding hands with twins. He explains things to them: 'There's a recession on, you see. That's why we're marching. We hope it'll help us.'

The two pensioners have continued chattering. 'But you only have to look. It's true, there *were* a lot more old folks than youngsters. It's like a church service.'

The thirty-something falls silent, one of the twins doesn't want to go any further.

The pensioners continue: 'Before, you had an education,

you were all trained up together. Politics meant something.'
They each pick up where the other leaves off. 'And another
thing, over the past few years, people have stopped demonstrating: they just go out for a nice stroll. What are they
waiting for? They need to make themselves heard. In our
day we'd never have come down from Mondeville without
pockets full of stones.'

The thirty-something tells the twins, 'It's when it starts
to hurt, like a football match when you lose. Get it?' Then
he turns to the pensioners. 'Dad, Mum, I'm going to have to
head for home.'

'Won't you come back to ours and have a quick drink
before lunch? Celebrate the demo?'

An unemployed worker from the association informs me
that, next week, there's perhaps going to be more action,
outside a Pôle Emploi office, near the Memorial. He's not
sure he'll be taking part himself. He can feel his anger
rising – he's had it up to here, and he rolls his eyes as he
holds his hand at throat level. 'I'm afraid I won't be able
to control myself.' He starts breathing heavily, as if short
of air. It's that time of confusion when the people in the
streets fold up their banners and the dining rooms unfold
their tablecloths. The unemployed chap gazes at the crowd.
'At least 80% of that lot don't have any great liking for us
unemployed.'

On the tram home, the demonstrators have heated argu-
ments about the shops where you can pick up the cheapest
tins of tuna. One woman is vexed. 'I'll tell you this much, at

Lidl's it's 55 centimes, and at Champion's it's 83. There's no comparing.'

'This is where I get off,' interrupts the other woman. I get off too. The tram moves away. We're alone on the pavement, which suddenly seems desperately empty after the crowds just now.

'Well, we're not staying here. Why don't you come and have a cup of coffee at mine?'

Victoria must be seventy or thereabouts. She's been a cleaner all her life, and this puts the seal on our friendship.

Victoria lives out towards the Vaucelles district, behind the station, the old railway workers' suburb, now peacefully becoming more gentrified. Along the streets, every house has its own little garden and every little garden a hedge around it, apparently planted and trimmed specially to allow the neighbours to stand on tiptoe, peer over the hedge, and wave a greeting. Between her lilac and her seringa, Victoria keeps three hens and a rabbit; the rabbit is regularly replaced by another, but its name is always the same, Roger.

With her dimples, and her short fringe, Victoria looks a bit like those pretty pioneer women who smiled out at their radiant future on the workers' posters of the sixties. But you have to be careful with her. Victoria can be a redoubtable women. She suggests heating up some coffee for me. There's some apple tart. She asks, 'Would you like some?'

Victoria comes from a quite different area, a village in the Manche, about sixty miles down the coast from Caen, towards Mont Saint-Michel. Victoria didn't like school. She didn't like picking potatoes, or cutting and removing the corn harvest from the beetroot, or any of the agricultural labour which her two brothers got through. She didn't like going to the beach, because in those days that meant picking up seaweed in the winter and lichen in the summer. Victoria liked having a ride on the fairground roundabouts with Nénette, who would later become a worker at Villedieu and buy herself a mobile home. Nénette and Victoria liked sharing a bike, their feet propped up on the handlebars, when it was time to come home and milk the cows. They liked having a laugh, and they laughed at the people who called them little hussies.

At the farm, they sow wheat and alfalfa. They have a dozen animals, mainly cows and two pigs; the family is respected. One morning, Victoria's father sends her to get her things ready, a woolly camisole, two pairs of pants, two handkerchiefs. He informs her, 'You're going to your aunt's, for a holiday.' Victoria doesn't really know her aunt, who runs a pork butcher's near Lisieux. She'd like to say goodbye to her mother, but her mother isn't there. She hugs the pet dog, goes to the door and, in front of the shelf where Our Lady of Lourdes is folding her plaster hands between photos of her first communion, Victoria kneels down. At the door, her father is talking to her aunt. She hears him asking, 'What are you going to pay her?' The aunt replies, 'She'll have enough for her food.' She's fifteen.

In her kitchen in Caen, Victoria asks me if I've ever been to Lisieux. 'Would you like me to show you?'

We drive east across the Auge region. Meadows full of cows are followed by meadows full of apples, and sometimes a fine big low-roofed farm sits between them. In the village, the high street has stayed the same, a few shops, the houses of the main families, with impressive gardens in front of them. The butcher's is under new management. Victoria presses her face to the shop window. 'That's not the way I used to do things.'

In those days, the evening stroll in the village consisted of watching the express train from Paris to Caen speed by, near the railway station. Once a year there was a ball in the courtyard of the town hall.

Victoria serves the customers in the butcher's and does the cleaning. Sometimes she's allowed to borrow Colette's bike – Colette is her cousin, she's at boarding school. The two girls are the same age. The family dreams of Colette becoming a teacher, and so she will. One Sunday, Victoria's aunt says to her, 'Do ask your cousin to give you a hand.' Colette is listening to jazz on the radio, sprawled on one chair, her feet on another. She starts to laugh, with that elegant, brazen laugh she has kept ever since. 'Give you a hand? You've got to be kidding. Can't you see how my mother's exploiting you?'

The better families in the village shop at the aunt's butcher's. Victoria scrutinizes the fingernails of the notary's wife every time she pays for the joint – nails that are lacquered with an almost transparent pink varnish, and immaculately manicured. They look like candies. Victoria has never seen anything so perfect.

This is the woman Victoria decides to ask one fine day whether there might not perhaps be any 'activities for young girls' in the village. The notary's wife sends her to see the priest, who runs a group of Jeunesse Ouvrière Chrétienne.* She hisses a warning to her: 'Watch out for this priest, though – he's a Red.' Victoria strikes up a friendship with the doctor's maid and the women workers from the factory opposite: Pierrette, who's marrying a policeman from Argentan; Jacqueline; and a huge red-headed girl nicknamed Tarzan, who's already had a child – nobody knows who the father is. Victoria joins the JOC. She is introduced to several girls who are employed in poor, overworked households. Victoria says that it's the job for her. A new future opens up for her: she'll be a social worker, too, and at last she'll be able to get away from the village.

Victoria struggles to explain how it is that she's still in Caen. 'We didn't ask ourselves so many questions in those days. You followed the railway line from out of our villages and got off in some city.' There, you live with girl friends, you rent some cramped little place near the station, you have dinner in secret in each other's rooms or sometimes get a hot meal from the nuns in the rue de l'Oratoire. You get bored out of your mind, you don't know what to do on a Sunday once you've polished your room and washed your clothes, you go to the cinema, you send money to your family, your

---

* An association for young Christians, mainly drawn from the working classes.

parents say it can pay for your bed sheets when you get married. The girls are almost all domestic cleaners.

Victoria joins a union. 'In 1959, when you were a social worker, people said, "You join." It was self-evident. Some women didn't, of course, especially those who kept an eye on their money.' Victoria is twenty-two.

The other day, right near her home, in the Vaucelles district, Victoria heard an old woman telling others at the tram stop: 'Okay girls, let's be going.' All of a sudden, she felt that her whole youth was coming back to her, the days when they called each other 'lads' and 'girls'.

6

The Advert

Everybody had warned me. If you come across a small ad for a job on the ferry at Ouistreham, be careful. Don't go. Don't reply to it. Don't even think of it. Forget it. Among the people I met, nobody had worked there, but they all said the same thing: that place is worse than all the rest, worse than the Turkish building companies, which pay you even less than in Turkey and sometimes don't even pay you at all; worse than the oyster farmers, who make you wait for hours between tides before going to shake the nets out at sea, whatever the weather; worse than market gardening, which does your back in for chicory or carrots; worse than the underground caves in Fleury, the old stone quarries that were turned into air-raid shelters during the war and that have now become mushroom beds that leave you feeling completely bushed at the end of an afternoon's work. As for apples, they make you sweat blood for them too, but the season starts later. Those jobs are like being in a penal colony and a prison hulk at the same time. But they're all better than the Ouistreham ferry.

Like every morning, I've just arrived at Pôle Emploi. I'm a

creature of habit now, I know which printer works properly, the telephone where you can almost get a bit of privacy, the right way to change the paper in the photocopying machine. I generally walk straight in, and try to grab the only computer where you can read the ads sitting down rather than standing at a narrow counter. Today it's free. It must be a providential sign, I'm sure.

I take off my hat, place my coat over the back of the chair, carefully, because it's often damp. I take out a biro, a piece of paper, and the huge pink plastic file with transparent dividers where I put the documents concerning 'my situation'. All the unemployed have one, even those who can't read or write. It's what marks us out. There are even some people who measure the time and energy that others have devoted to job-hunting simply from the size and organization of their files, like those biologists who can determine the age of cockchafers from the size of their joints.

At reception, a guy who's dripping with sweat is protesting. 'I know I haven't made an appointment, but I'd just like to ask you to erase my telephone number from my file. I'm worried that an employer will give up if he tries to phone and there's no answer.'

'Why?' asks the receptionist – today it's a slim young blonde.

'It's stopped working.'

'What's stopped working?'

'My phone.'

'Why's it stopped working?'

'They've cut me off for financial reasons.'

'But you can't turn up here just like that. You need to make an appointment.'

'Okay, let's keep calm. I'll start again: I'd like to make an appointment, please, Miss.'

The young blonde woman appears sincerely annoyed. 'I'm so sorry, Sir. We no longer make appointments face to face. It's not our fault, it's the new regulations, we have to apply them. Try to see it from our point of view. Appointments have to made by phone these days.'

'But my phone doesn't work.'

'There are telephones for you to use at the far end of the agency, but I must warn you: you need to phone just one number, 39-49, which gets you through to a central office they've just set up. It's always being bombarded by customers. You can be waiting for ages.'

'Ages?'

'Sometimes for several hours.'

Around my chair, my coat has traced little rivulets of water on the ground. This morning, I'm waiting for answers about a job as a cleaner in a health centre, as a night guard in a hotel in Caen, as a cleaner in a perfume shop in the Mondeville-2 shopping centre, and as a saleswoman in a garden centre. On the computer, the program that looks for offers corresponding to my file has started up; they're mainly for cleaning jobs, some jobs in sales, seasonal work . . . basically, they're all temporary things that don't require any qualifications. Some days there aren't any more than a score of these jobs for the whole of Basse-Normandie. I tend to prefer the ones that specify 'beginners accepted': they make me feel that doors are opening and something's actually turning up. But this almost never happens. For days, I haven't seen a single offer for a full-time job, for a permanent contract, or a wage above the minimum legally possible. An employee at Pôle Emploi told me that this was to be expected. 'This type of work just doesn't exist any more in your particular sector. Soon these jobs won't exist anywhere, perhaps. Nobody knows.'

As I gaze, the day's offers have started to come up on screen. I know almost all of them off by heart, they're the same that have been going the rounds for days, sometimes.

'In Deauville, you will clean the exterior of a luxury shop, pavements and windows included. You will work 1½ hours per day, Monday to Saturday, from 9 to 10.30 a.m. Experience in window cleaning required.'

'In Bréville, in a community building, you will be an adaptable person who can wait at table, wash up, and clean shared areas and bedrooms. Split timetable (9 a.m.–2.30 p.m. and 7.30–10 p.m.), work on holidays and at weekends in rotation; no accommodation provided, fixed period contract for two months, experience waiting at table, food provided.'

'In Mondeville, you will clean a house in the Étoile ZAC,* Tuesdays and Wednesdays from 9.30 to 10.30 a.m., you will wash the floors, you will do the dusting, you will disinfect the

---

* ZAC: *Zone d'aménagement concerté*, an area set aside by local government for specific planning projects.

bathroom and toilet, you will empty the bins. The ability to clean windows with a squeegee is an advantage. Dynamism, independence, meticulousness, speed, experience required, must be able to read and write. Limited-period contract for two days, two hours maximum.'

'In Caen, rue Guillaume-le-Conquérant, at Quick Horse, you will need to be able to make pizzas, deliver them by scooter, maintain the premises, work 7/7, timetable from 11.30 a.m. to 2.30 p.m. and from 6 to 11 p.m. Minimum wage.'

'In Honfleur, you will clean the rooms of a hotel, meeting hygiene standards, you will need to be available for breakfast from 5.30 a.m. No accommodation provided, English required, must have 2 years' experience in a similar position.'

'In Ifs, you will be responsible for various handling tasks, mowing the lawn, maintenance and small repairs, delivery of car parts. Your contract will be for 5 months, position reserved for handicapped employees.'

'In Merville-Franceville-Plage, you will guarantee the spotless cleanliness of the establishment, you will be responsible for cleaning the bathrooms and toilets, the mobile homes and all the reception areas. Contract for 4 hours per week for four months.'

I spot another ad.

'In Caen, you will take part in a round of events of national importance. Urgent.'

*

I phone and – amazingly – it's not engaged. The man who picks up the phone introduces himself as the 'manager'. He explains that the round of events consists in handing out samples of deodorant on a pedestrian street in the town centre, one Saturday afternoon. 'Are you over twenty-five? So why are you wasting my time? You know that's a negative point for this kind of work. And what do you look like? Blond hair? Red hair? What style? Glamour girl? Rock singer? I warn you, I've got a pile of applicants in front of me: one more negative point and I'm hanging up.'

In the entrance hall of Pôle Emploi, the queue keeps swaying gently in time with the heavy sighs of a person I can't identify. Behind me, there's a girl laughing as she makes a phone call. I know her, or at least I bump into her here every day. She's in a good mood that nothing can cloud. 'We're going to have to pay Électricité de France 20 euros. But I promise you, Mum, I'd started to lower the heating to 15 degrees. I didn't want to freeze to death so I put it back up to 18. I'm still cold, but I don't dare put it any higher.' She's still laughing. At the local job office, they've just suggested she take a professional *bac*, specializing in 'sales of sports equipment'. She's said yes. It'll mean two years' wages, at least that's what she understood, because the man was talking very fast. 'I'd rather have worked in a canteen, like you, but I didn't dare say so.' She laughs again and her teeth crunch on a chocolate-coated peanut that she's fished out of a packet in front of her. 'Anyway, it'll do for today, don't you worry. I've borrowed 3 euros from

Sandrine. I'll sort out something else tomorrow. Love you, Mum.'

It's at just that minute that the two brief lines come up on my screen.

Cleaning agency at Ouistreham seeks employees (m. or f.) to work on ferries. Beginners accepted.

There it is, the long-awaited small ad. I phone straight-away, I can't resist. I have to turn up the next day, at 9.30 a.m., at business headquarters, on the Quai Charcot in Ouistreham, with ID and a colour photo.

The next day, white clouds have shrouded everything, not exactly in fog, rather in a gauze-thin mist which seems to muffle every sound and through which there emerges, from time to time, a little boat or a cyclist. The Quai Charcot in Ouistreham follows the canal from Caen to where it flows out into the English Channel. The business premises are here, just upstream from the sea. There's a tiny poodle bark-ing. 'Quiet, Napoleon!' calls a reedy voice. In 1857, Empress Eugénie and Napoleon III opened the eight and a half miles of the canal and its two locks, which were supposed to make the fortune of the port of Ouistreham by linking it to the nas-cent industrial estate of Caen. For generations, pets, boats, and mobile homes have been given one of these prestigious imperial names – which alone keep alive the memory of the event and, even more, the memory of its faded ambitions.

The neon sign of an off-licence for lorry drivers shines out onto the quay like a lighthouse. Opposite, a score of old fishing smacks are tied up at their moorings; a little illegal

port, nicknamed Hong Kong, from where the last buccaneers
head out to fish for bass or scallops. Much further along, completely out of sight from here, is the other Ouistreham, with
its casino and its Riva Bella beach, where Italian ice-cream
wrappers are typical of family afternoons out, on Sundays
when it's not raining.

The company premises look like the boat sheds around
them, low-roofed and functional. In the entrance hall, a guy
with a cider-coloured moustache is bawling out one applicant. 'That's twice you've been here looking for work. The
first time, you had problems with your schedule and your car.
Have you sorted them yet? No? So why've you come back,
then? Goodbye. The rest of you, sit round the table.'

There are a dozen of us, a mixture of men and women.
It soon turns out that the fellow with the moustache can
only be the boss, the 'big boss' as I'll hear him referred to
later on, or – more respectfully – by his first name alone,
'Jeff', which the people who work on the ferry (especially the
more humble among them) like to drag into their conversations. Jeff lives in another town, over sixty miles away from
Ouistreham. Every day, before dawn, he has a two-hour drive
to get to the port by daybreak, just before the docking of the
first ferry, which has also had a long journey – from England.

In public, Jeff can mimic the employees very realistically
– he even captures the way they walk and talk. It's a highly
valued source of entertainment. He challenges them, teases
them, lays into them, congratulates them, and protects them
in turn.

Jeff sometimes goes on board the ferry during the hours of service – he has a marked preference for the morning sessions. There's always someone to spread the word of his visits. 'By the way, Jeff came in today.' 'Oh? And?' 'Oh, nothing' comes the almost unvarying reply, but in the way this 'nothing' is pronounced there's just a hint – even if the mystery is never explained – that the day won't have been altogether the same for the people who have crossed his path.

Jeff gazes at us, one after the other, as we sit round the table. Nobody has dared take off their coat, and one guy has even kept his crash helmet and his motorbike gloves on, as if expecting to be turned away like the other applicant – so abruptly that he'll need to make a quick getaway. 'You get out your ID and I'll make some photocopies. You'll be trained up tomorrow morning, and you start the day after. Usually there are three ferries per day, at 6 a.m., 2 p.m., and half nine in the evening. You do the cleaning while the ship's in port, between the time the boat docks and the time it sets sail. Initially, you'll be employed on the evening timetable, six days a week, Wednesdays off. The onboard shift is till half ten in the evening. That's an hour paid at basic salary. After that, we'll see. No questions?'

We hand over our ID.

'One last thing,' says Jeff. 'If you come from Caen, you'll need a car: there's no bus corresponding to your schedule. So my advice is that you get together to share petrol costs, otherwise you'll waste your whole pay packet on fuel: you'll be getting just over 250 euros per month, with bonuses on holidays and Sundays.' He waves our papers in front of him, fan-shaped, like a hand of cards. 'No regrets? Everyone got the message? Nobody got cold feet?' He looks at me. 'You got a car?' I lie straight off. 'Yes, of course.' Jeff keeps looking at me. 'If you say so.'

He writes our names down, and hands our ID back. 'You can go now.' So that's that. Sorted. We've signed up for six months, it all lasted ten minutes and, apart from Jeff, I can remember hardly any of those who were with me round the table.

Before I started job-hunting in Caen, this was just how I'd imagined that getting work would feel like – as simple and brutal as hiring casual labour. But now I can't get over it, it's been amazingly easy, I've finally got through the series of tasks and the ritual genuflections required even for a temporary one-week job. In the bus home, I even start wondering whether it's true, whether I have actually been hired.

I still need to find a car for the next day. I first think of Philippe. We've phoned one another a couple of times since that lunch in Bayeux and, just as he answers the phone, I remember he doesn't have any means of transport. I tell myself it's silly to phone him, but we catch up a bit. Philippe always has a good story to tell – it's one of the nice things about him. This time, he's just signed a contract – 'three months in parks and gardens' – and he asks me round for Sunday. If I say yes straightaway, he'll do his special veal Orloff for me. He could also borrow a motorbike from one of his card-playing partners so we can go out together one evening, 'to a wrestling match, maybe. What d'you reckon?'

He thinks he needs to promise me something as quickly as possible, to make up for the car problem which he can't sort. 'You'll be the first woman I've taken to the Caen fair this spring.' Last year he almost won an iPhone at one of the lottery booths, the one right next to the main road. 'Can you imagine? I was a hair's breadth away from getting my hands on it – I could have called you with it today. It'll be great to go together.' While he talks, I can't stop thinking about the car. He realizes as much and rams the point home. 'If I was you, I'd be really worried about not getting one. If you don't sort it, you're a goner. As far as a place to live goes, they never ask any questions, you can sleep under the bridges for all they care. But you can't do without a car. I thought you'd be a bit quicker on the uptake. Everybody knows you need a car.' He pauses. 'Yep, you need to get your butt into gear and find one.' He repeats: 'Or else you're a goner.'

I can't help thinking I'm going to screw up the first, maybe the only job I'm going to get. All of a sudden, I find Philippe really annoying. I tell him, 'What about you? You don't have a car either! How do you manage?'

'In my case it was either divorce or a car. I couldn't afford both. We split up just like that, without thinking about it, but since then I really can't manage with the money from the divorce. I nearly went back to live with my parents. Anyway, while we're talking of jobs, d'you want to know the truth? The whole truth and nothing but the truth? The three-month contract I told you about, it's not actually in parks and gardens. I told you that to impress you, I thought it sounded classy, nice and eco-friendly. Actually, I'll be packing eggs into their boxes in a factory. Before, for nearly a year, I unloaded lorry-loads of animals at the abattoir, and before that I filleted fish, I stank of the sea for months. And I might not even have got all that work without my left eye, you know, the one that means I get better treatment because of my disability.'

'Ah, the one that women go for.'

Philippe laughs. 'At all events, I've given up my ideas of a career. So there it is.'

'What kind of career?'

'I wanted to set up my own business.'

'What in?'

'I don't really like to talk about it, but I trust you. I know, it was a crazy idea, too big for me, but I'd have hung on in there. I wanted a van, my own van, to sell pizzas from. Don't get me wrong, you know: not fries, and not hot dogs – pizzas.'

I've really *got* to find a car. I can think of only one person who can save my skin: Victoria. I rush over to the Vaucelles district. Victoria is sorting out paperwork on the dining-room table, putting it into little piles in front of her. She's drawing up lists of things she needs to do, people to phone. She's heard that a couple of friends of hers want to sell an old car they don't need any more. They're in no hurry, they could lend it me for a few weeks, it would tide me over before I give it back. We head off to see it straightaway. Its owners have nicknamed it 'the Tractor' because of the noise it makes and the way it looks: it's a bottle-green Fiat, diesel engine, 1992, with a child seat in the rear. I can't help hugging its owners.

7

The Toilets

It's very early in the morning. Yesterday, to make sure I wouldn't be late, I did the journey twice in the Tractor, my new car. We're supposed to get there at 5.30 a.m., at the ferry embarkation port, for the morning training session. As I exit Caen, a few lorries are gently edging onto the expressway between the roundabouts and the speed traps, as if they were weightless; others are still parked like herds at the turn-off into the towns, where they've spent the night.

In Ouistreham, a lorry driver is having a wash in the water trough for the horses – big sorrels in the middle of a meadow, between the expressway and the shopping centre. Something Philippe said keeps going round and round in my head. I'd told him that absolutely everyone had advised me not to work on a ferry. Philippe had laughed. 'Do you think you've got any choice?'

It's really early, not 5 o'clock yet, when I drive past the company premises along the canal. The landing stage is further on, right at the end of the jetty. On a small square, a shooting range and the merry-go-round of a miniature funfair glitter in the dark. Opposite, a market where fish are auctioned off looks so clean and empty that it seems like another fairground attraction. At the far end of a deserted car park, there aren't any lights on yet in the terminal of the harbour station.

In front of the checkpoint which controls the customs area, a man and a woman hug in the darkness, kitted out in oversized fluorescent yellow jackets that flap in the wind like Halloween costumes. On its slender stand, their scooter looks like a toy. The introductions don't take long. Her name is Marilou, she's twenty and, usually, she's the one who speaks on behalf of the two of them. When she gestures to the young man, she says 'my boyfriend', then stamps her feet noisily, because it's cold and the soles of her trainers have split. She's waiting for the sales so she can buy some new ones. Like me, she's just been hired. But her boyfriend hasn't. He's come with her because he doesn't know what to do without her. He gets bored. In their couple, it's Marilou who wears the trousers.

Right away, she asks me the question that's nagging away at her. 'Any idea where you can get a joint of meat a bit cheaper?' Her parents live in Condé-sur-Noireau. They come to have lunch with her on a Sunday. It's a grand occasion.

Marilou and her boyfriend live in Caen: they've taken almost an hour with their fluorescent jackets and their tiny scooter, struggling against the gusts of wind to travel the nine miles by road. We don't know each other very well, but we fling ourselves into each other's arms. Yes, we can share cars, as Jeff recommended. Yes, I'll come and pick her up every day. Yes, we'll be bosom pals from now on. Yes, we feel we've been saved because each of us has just noticed in the other's eyes the same anxiety about having to launch into the fierce world of the ferry. Her exaltation wavers a little when she asks me where I've parked. Her eyes fall on the Tractor, still steaming and trembling after its journey, all alone in the car park. She doesn't say anything, but I can sense that I'm being judged severely and that only the absolute necessity of this job will get her to accept the idea of being seen in that con-traption every day. Marilou doesn't have her driver's licence, or a car, but you'd have thought she'd been brought up to survive in a supermarket car park. From a distance, just by listening, she can recognize a car more easily than any human being, and she's able to recite all the makes and prices of all the car dealers in town; she already knows which car she's going to buy – and with what extras – when she's got a bit of money (in other words, very soon). Anyway, it's going to be a new car, that's for sure.

There are five of us new employees at the landing stage today.

We need to make a new trip to get to the ferry. We need to get into the customs zone by showing a badge with our photo, as provided by the company. Sometimes, guards emerge from their site offices to hunker down and check out the axles or the passenger compartments, muttering about trafficking and illegal immigrants. We take up our stations outside a building composed of a small bare room flanked by two toilets. We wait for the company coach that will take us to the ferry. The distance between the two must not exceed seven hundred yards or so, but it's forbidden to walk this distance. With the wait, the coach journey, and the new wait before going on board, you need to add on a good half hour.

The other employees arrive on the quay one by one, maybe forty of them, mainly girls, a few men too. Nobody's had enough sleep; they are all wrapped in the last haze of slumber, their lowered faces colourless and still crumpled by night, their hair unkempt. They exchange few words, not even to ask for a cigarette. When one takes out a packet, there are begging glances, hands are held out, and heads are nodded in silent thanks, sometimes with a snuffle. People move in quick shivers, tremulous and stiff, tensed up against the damp that they can feel ready to sidle in between the layers of their clothes every time they shift position, like icy fingers clutching at their warm skin. Some of us breathe a quick 'hello', but 'a severe hello', as Marilou whispers, always on the alert. We are all wearing the green and white striped overalls with the company logo on them. It is forbidden to go on board with anything except your badge, and a biro that allows you to sign the attendance sheet.

On an electronic notice-board, brilliant green letters write on the dark of the sky: 'Calm sea, little swell.' We sense, rather than see, at the end of the quay, a silent shadow in a lighter grey, with the occasional trail of white foam.

The coach arrives.

On the boarding steps, huddled against the guardrail,

we wait for the passengers to exit before we can move in.
Soon, I'll have stopped paying them any attention, absorbed
much more in this new world that I am to inhabit. But this
is my first day and I can't stop staring at all these people with
their suitcases, to whom I conscientiously wish a resound-
ing 'Welcome to France!' Nobody replies. Sometimes, one of
them looks at me, as amazed as if the bundle of rope coiled on
the deck had started to speak to him. I've become invisible.

The ferry has adopted the style of a cruise liner for the
masses. Everything is there, in the right place, shiny bright
and highly polished, as tradition requires: the brass, the
varnished wood, the fitted carpets, the copperware, the
upholstered armchairs, the bar and its choice of drinks. But
the sensations that should go along with all this – the hush of
mellow comfort – are missing. The lorry drivers' menu in the
restaurant offers as many fries as you can eat (it's self-service),
and the old posters vaunting the Mother-of-Pearl Coast are
mere reproductions.

Mauricette is in charge of the crew, and she's been picked
to train us. She has very short hair, platinum blond, and a
physique that's just right for the job. Her temper rises and
falls like the sea and nobody knows which Mauricette will
reply when we address her. She likes this. And she makes the
most of it.

Marilou and I are still joined at the hip: we try not to make
any gaffes. 'You two, over there, you're going to do the *sanis*.'
This is the first word I learn on board. *Sanis* means the sani-
tary arrangements, and this phrase in turn means 'toilets'. To

do the *sanis* is to clean the toilets, the main – and exclusively female – job on board. Sometimes, a male employee is told, 'You're doing the *sanis*,' but this never actually happens, it's always just a tease, even with the rebels and the scapegoats. The men do the vacuuming and the carpet cleaning, they spruce up the restaurants and the bars, and set up the bunks for the night crossings. They never, ever rub down the toilet pans.

So today we are going to be trained to do the *sanis* in the passenger cabins. Mauricette hands us a plastic basket with two sprays and a score of cleaning cloths, then we follow her at the double down the first of the ferry's endless corridors – this one is so narrow that you have to flatten yourself against the wall when someone else comes past. The cabins are all on the one side, about every six feet or so. Mauricette opens the door to the first one and dashes into the tiny space where four bunks are fitted over each other and there's a boxroom toilet which itself includes a washbasin, a shower, and the toilets. She drops down to the ground, so suddenly that I initially think she's stumbled over something. I go forward to help her up but, without even glancing behind her, she shakes herself to push me away and, on her knees on the tiles, starts to aim her spray at everything in sight, from the floor to the ceiling. Then, still squatting down, she crumples, dries, disinfects, polishes, changes the toilet paper and the bins, arranges the bars of soap and the tumblers in an immaculate row over the washbasin, and checks the shower curtain. It's all taken less than three minutes: that's the time allowed for this task.

Mauricette dashes out of the toilets. In the cabin, she dusts everything that can be dusted, makes the mirrors shine, and picks up the waste paper (thirty seconds). At the same time and in the same space, at least two other employees are busy, changing the sheets in the bunks (they call this 'bunking up') and running the vacuum round (they call this 'vaccing up'). They all manage to avoid each other, their arms and legs come within a fraction of an inch, the sheets fly about at head height but never touch anyone, all in perfect timing: the frenzy shown by every employee in his or her task, and the restricted space, make this achievement particularly spectacular. One of the girls is singing 'Il jouait du piano debout',* others join in the rhythm with a swing of their hips.

Mauricette turns round. 'Everything's got to be spotless. Take special care you don't leave a single hair behind, don't forget to use a different coloured cloth for the toilets and to sponge away every drop in the shower, especially if it's been used recently, and remember not to leave any bit of used soap and to chuck out all the rolls of toilet paper that have been started.' I forget all of this straightaway: I'm in a state of alarm bordering on panic. When Mauricette announces, 'Okay, off you go,' I almost throw up. She gives us all a big smile. 'You're lucky, she's in a good mood,' says one girl.

In a quarter of an hour, my knees have doubled in volume, my arms have pins and needles, and I'm in a real muck-sweat in the pullover that I decided it would be a good idea to keep

* A well-known pop song.

on. I can't stop bumping into people and furniture; I narrowly avoid poking the eye out of a colleague with a spray while she's bunking up. She keeps her cool. 'The month I started, I had cramp all over my body. I lost at least a stone.'

At regular intervals I hear Mauricette's cry behind me, piercing through the hubbub of the gangway. 'Flooooooreeeeence!' This means I've screwed up. 'Come here. See anything in the shower? The hairs, there, on the side?' I have to start rubbing away in front of her, on all fours in the *sanis*, while she continues to spur on the rest of the troop, without looking behind her. 'Come on, girls, move it, you need to keep up the rhythm. You're not finished yet.' I set off in the other direction, ashen-faced, though I can't help feeling a vague sense of relief when I realize that the person I've just knocked over is the only one I know, Marilou. The change in her appearance is stupefying. 'Hey, you're so red! And soaking! You like you've been through the wringer.'

She's indignant. 'You haven't seen yourself. You're purple. I'd hardly have recognized you.'

Everywhere people are running, telling jokes, snitching, giving each other a hand: there's a never-ending hustle and bustle, and a constant din – a clatter of buckets colliding, water running, vacuum cleaners roaring. Today, everyone's laying into 'Stinkball', a woman who's very small and very plump and has the reputation of never washing. Her name flies across the corridors, bellowed from one cabin to the next. 'Have you seen the *sanis* that Stinkball's just done?' – 'Disgusting.' – 'It was cleaner before she came along.' – 'Hey,

Stinkball, where are you?' – 'She's over there, I can smell her.'
– 'You can follow her from the smell.' – 'Oh, I've just bumped
into her, so I pulled the chain.' They laugh. Then they sing,
'Stinkball, Stinkball,' then they come face to face with her
and everyone joins in the fun, sniggering insolently. It carries
on further down the corridor: 'If you catch Stinkball, push
her under the shower and turn on the tap.'

The young girls call the older girls 'old gal'. The old gals
call the younger ones 'scumbags'. The men aren't called anything – they are treated with an indulgence that sometimes
borders on contempt. And they don't venture to open their
mouths too much, except when they're flirting.

The hour lasts a second and an eternity. As I sign the
attendance sheets, I can finally make out the faces around me.
All human life is here on the ferry: attractive women, ugly
women, women who are practically down and out, mothers,
little peasants, whores and high-class models. But we all rub
shoulders and jostle along in a sort of sisterly togetherness
that is made easier by us all having to wear a uniform and
knuckle down to hard work.

A really pretty young girl, with a body piercing placed like
a beauty spot on the edge of her lip, asks me what shift I've
been given. 'The evening,' I tell her. She seems to think this
is a piece of good luck. She tells me, 'You'll see, there's a different atmosphere. There's something unhealthy about the
afternoons, though you get used to it. Mornings are really
horrible. The only thing that brightens it up is seeing the old
gals without their war paint on.'

I drive Marilou home to celebrate the way we've hitched up together. She's already got two jobs in cleaning, on fixed-term contracts – 'of course', as she points out. There's the morning job, the one she likes best; she'd like to 'wangle a permanent contract' for this one. She lists the good things about it. 'The boss is nice. There's not too much to do. There's nobody hassling you.' It's from 6.30 to 8.30 a.m., in a superstore before it opens. In the evening, from 6.45 to 8.00 p.m., she cleans offices at Youpi-Métal. Her superior asked to see her the other day. 'You're making calls on your mobile phone during working hours, you're talking to your colleagues. We're going to let you go.' Marilou received a letter that she didn't really understand. It eventually emerged that she had to go and explain her behaviour at the Youpi-Métal headquarters in Lisieux. Her boyfriend shrugged. He can't read. Lisieux by train is dear, and a long way by scooter. The appointment was for 9 a.m., which didn't give her any time to finish her first job. The whole business seemed to her too complicated and expensive. The boss dangled in front of her the idea that the payslip looks better if you leave a job. 'You'll immediately pick up a wage adjustment for paid holidays, and some of the bonuses. That'll give you at least 200 euros more, a sort of golden parachute, if you like.' Marilou allowed herself to be kicked out. 'It's still money, isn't it?' She signed up for the ferry.

Together, we work out how to arrive on time. From Caen, the journey takes half an hour. To catch the coach that takes us to the ferry, we need to be at the harbour by 9 p.m. In other words, we've got roughly an hour to get from place to place and then hang around, in both directions. Since only the time spent on board is paid, two hours are lost for the sake of one. Marilou's face doesn't register any annoyance. I ask her, 'Do you think it's wasting too much time for the wages we're earning?' She doesn't understand. Where've I been all this time if I don't know this is the way it usually is? For her morning job, she has to travel for three hours.

8

Teeth

I've spotted an ad in a shopping centre. Cleaning again, but this time in a fast-food joint. 'Can you be here in a quarter of an hour? I'll show you around.'

I'm just parking the Tractor when I hear someone banging at the car window. A female employee in uniform is waiting for me between the puddles. Two plaits of hair emerge from her little hat, and her pink bare legs glisten in the rain. They look like sticks of barley sugar. She says, 'Actually, the job's already taken.' In the shopping arcade, there are people sitting down, each one with a trolley whose prow is pointed towards the doors of the hypermarket. They're waiting for it to open. It's 8.45 a.m. 'Another three quarters of an hour,' someone announces.

On the coast, towards Colleville, a holiday camp is looking for 'all-purpose female workers'. The manageress greets me as if I were a friend who's called round to take tea with her. 'Good Lord! You've driven all the way from Caen? You must be exhausted.' The sound of our clattering footsteps echoes through the empty building, with its musty-smelling dormitories, to the courtyard, with its leafless trees. In a tiled, completely white room, short rectangular aluminium tables sparkle in the harsh neon light. I ask, 'Is this the sick bay?'

'No, the pantry.'

The hygiene regulations forbid any cooking. You're not allowed to touch anything with your bare hands, neither the food nor the children. The food comes in by lorry, vacuum packed, ready-prepared – even the raw vegetables. Then, armour-plated in overalls, gloves, slippers, with mob caps on our heads and masks over our mouths, we need to decant what's in the containers onto plates that we then serve out in the dining hall, still dressed in the same garb.

Before, during, and after, the buildings have to be scrubbed from 7 a.m. to 2 p.m., with an unpaid break – which you can take whenever. You start again from 6 to 9.30 p.m. 'It's a schooling in flexibility, all for the sake of the kiddies,' the manageress concludes, clapping her hands. She has no idea of how many hours per week, or the type of contract, or the wages, but she's sure I'll have to work weekends and holidays. She wants someone who'll show willing, that's all. She sighs, 'If such a thing's still possible in France'.

I'm available at all times, every day, for any task, and it seems to me like a good idea to repeat this fact several times, in a determined tone of voice. The only limit on my time is my work on the ferry. I could give this up if the new contract were better, but I'd need more details. The manageress is aggrieved at my attitude. She tells me so. 'It's difficult for me, too. You don't realize. You're too busy gazing at your

own navel. I often wonder what women like you are thinking. What are you after, deep down? They say there's a lot
of unemployment, but look, the fact is I can't find anybody.
Don't let me keep you, Madam.'

I've found another holiday camp that's also recruiting, further away, near the Normandy beaches. I fill up the car before
setting off, as I've decided to go there directly. The Tractor
first stalls, then refuses to emit so much as a squeak. Just as
I'm starting to get worried, it demurely springs back to life.
Under a liquid sky, the Tractor tootles along through this
part of Normandy, decked out as it is in allied flags and paper
lanterns, with traces of military activity scattered all around.
The atmosphere is a cross between a garrison and a dance
hall, as if the landings and the Liberation had just taken
place.

Every so often, a ray of light pierces through the rain and
makes a thick black streak on the horizon glimmer. It looks
like tar. It's the sea. In the villages, the bakeries are all sign-
posted in English. I can't find the holiday camp. A hotel
owner, who also rents out period military costumes, advises
me to follow the column of restored jeeps filled with octoge-
narian Americans heading off on a pilgrimage to the beaches.
'You go as far as the hypermarket and there you turn just after
the tank covered in bunches of plastic flowers. You go along
a sort of revamped military camp and pass the service station.
It's five hundred yards further on.'

I get there. The manageress is all charm. The job's already
taken.

I push the Tractor on to get back to Caen as fast as possible. Pôle Emploi have scheduled a workshop for me at the beginning of the afternoon: 'How to write your own résumé.'

On the agency car park, where the car doors are ajar, advisors are eating lunch, each in his or her own vehicle, with paper napkins spread out across the steering wheel. They're talking about a colleague who committed suicide in his agency, a few days earlier, in the Nord.

'Apparently, he hanged himself from the stairs at Pôle Emploi. The others found him when they arrived at eight in the morning.'

'The day before, he'd given the woman at the next desk a bunch of daffodils.'

'Here, in our agency, they say they're going to stop us accessing the Internet. I think they want to stop us hearing about this kind of thing.'

'One colleague says it looks like there've been several other suicide attempts. She's supposed to be phoning me to tell me more.'

'You watch out: they might be bugging the phones.'

'Yes, it's better if you phone from home.'

'You know they can prosecute you if you talk about Pôle Emploi to outsiders? I've heard that someone was hauled over the coals for speaking to the press.'

Everyone slams their car door.

Next to the entrance, two women are waiting for the same class as I am. The uncertain sun suddenly filters through a cloud.

'Did you do the "Unsolicited letter of application" course?' asks one of them.

'No, I tried the "Home help" module.'

She didn't get selected.

'They asked us questions about the government. I got 3 out of 20. I looked a proper twit.'

The other woman chokes. 'Questions on government? That's insulting! As if we knew anything about that!'

At the reception counter, a hubbub has broken out. 'Again!' sighs one of the two women. It's a forty-something man in a tie; his damp hair still bears the traces of a comb. None of us has picked up what he's after, and, to tell the truth, 'we don't give a damn', as the other woman puts it.

'What about the "Writing a letter of reply to a small ad" course? Have you done that one?'

'No, I did "Highlighting your skills".'

The first woman lowers her voice. 'Have you heard the rumours about these courses? Apparently, if you don't turn up, they can take you off the register.'

The woman at reception has started shouting in turn, so loud that our conversation has been interrupted yet again. Eventually we step inside the agency; it's started to rain.

'Go on then, punch me in the face, don't let me stop you!' shouts the receptionist.

The man in the tie yells even louder: 'Certainly not! I don't want to go to jail because of you! You'd be too glad to see me go!'

'Go on, go on, hit me, then it'll be done!'

The guy hesitates and then runs for it. He tries to find the exit door, gets it wrong, ends up in the corridor leading to the toilets. The other advisors, who'd been washing up the luncheon cutlery in the sinks, vamoose to the sound of cutlery crashing to the ground. The man in the tie locks himself into the women's toilets. In the entrance hall, they're unsure whether to enter the incident in the agency's 'security record'. 'Will we have more hassle if we mention it or if we don't?' One Pôle Emploi employee can't see what there is to record: he thinks it's only to be expected that job-seekers will fly off the handle, given the situation these days. Everyone ponders the matter. If the incident *is* recorded, the man in the tie will probably be punished.

The two women and I continue our little chat.

'What about the "Using the phone to find a job" course? Do you know about that one?'

'No, I did the "Cooking a balanced diet with a social services parcel", but I don't think that one was organized by Pôle Emploi.'

'All this stuff does take up a lot of time. It ends up being worse than a job.'

Suddenly there's a noise of banging from the toilets. It's the man with the tie again. He's got stuck in the women's toilet – he can't manage to unlock the door.

Our workshop begins.

There are supposed to be twelve of us, there are only nine; the session begins with the inevitable exercise of introducing ourselves to one another. A young girl, afflicted by a permanent helpless giggle, can't even manage to get her name out. A teenage boy with a big spider tattooed on his neck can't see any reason for telling his life story to strangers, or for learning how to write a résumé, or for giving it to potential employers. He's a pastrycook, and pastrycooks can recognize each other, they know what they're talking about in their own pastrycook language, without any need for a résumé. On his neck, the legs of the spider seem to start moving as he swells with anger. 'Nobody is being forced to stay here,' says the woman in charge of the workshop. She remains perfectly courteous and gazes at us; her eyes are big and pale, prominent and glistening. 'We're just offering you a bit of help, not an extra burden.'

One student is answering his mobile, without even bothering to lower his voice. 'No, no, you're not bothering me, I'm at a crap course. I'll be there in five minutes.' He leaves, as do Spiderman and the young girl with the giggles.

The course leader begins. 'Employers are inundated by unsolicited applications – they get hundreds of them. I'm not sure that skills is what they're mainly after. They're looking for someone who'll catch their eye. You need to get yourself noticed at all costs.' She seems to believe what she's saying.

The 'résumé' course is going to teach us how to camouflage gaps, problem areas, difficult periods, time out, lack of experience, the absence of specialization, and even blank résumés, the most unpromising, the ones where there's almost nothing. She stares at me with her pale eyes. 'Like yours.'

She gives us formulae that none of us would be able to

dream up for ourselves, such as 'varied experience' or 'transferable skills'. One woman who's worried she's going to forget it all asks me to write it down for her on the back of her bus pass.

The course leader continues. 'An employer will spend on average between thirty seconds and two minutes to read a résumé. Don't mention your financial or other problems, your divorces, or the times you were out of work. You need to make them want to meet you: you can't put down everything, even if it's true. Before mentioning a detail, remember that it might make the person reading you feel negative. If in doubt, don't.'

If the résumé is 'attractive', then you've won. But you have to be careful: 'won' doesn't mean you've got a job. 'You know, there just isn't any work right now,' she continues. Then she has second thoughts. 'Well, not much. "Won" means you've landed yourself an interview. This is already fantastic, a very valuable stage, but you need to have a thick skin. There'll be several people sitting opposite you. You need to get psyched up beforehand.'

She points to one of the two women who'd been chatting outside the door just now. 'What kind of thing are you looking for?'

'I used to run children's theatre workshops, for quite a while. Now I'm not sure.'

'Imagine an employer asking you why you've replied to his ad, what do you tell him?'

The woman sighs. 'I've applied because I'm out of work,

but I know that's not the right answer.' She pinches her lips, narrows her eyes, and mimes all the signs of intense concentration. Then, reassuming her usual expression, despairing over her own ignorance, she says, 'I don't know.'

'You're right, it's pointless telling them you're out of work. Everyone's out of work. And you mustn't say, "I like this job because it's not tiring," either. So, what do you think's the right answer? You, Madam, any idea?'

The course leader has just turned to a solemn, silent person, who's been sitting massively at the back of the room ever since the beginning of the course, her eyes like two slits swallowed up in her folds of flesh, black hair – though not much of it – pulled tight behind the head, and no teeth at all. When the course leader talks to her, she barely moves her head, as ageless as that of an Indian chieftain, as if she wished merely to shake off a fly that was bothering her.

The other persists. 'Well, Madam? Can you hear me, Madam? Madam? Madam? All right, I'll give you the answer: you need to sing the praises of the company, but also advertise your own merits. You need to say things like "I'm available at such-and-such a time." In particular, you need to show that you can adapt to a certain number of things. These days, if you're going to refuse to work on Sundays, you need to have been in the job for a long time already. Don't take any risks. Even if you can't do what they're asking, say that you can. You'll always get by somehow. Don't forget that you need to turn up at the interview all neat and tidy, and, most of all, be on time. These are the two things that employers mainly complain about. If you manage to end up among the best, you may be kept on, as temps. There's nothing else available for the time being.'

The other woman puts her hand up. 'I've listened to the information you give us here twice over. Is what we've heard true or not? Isn't there any kind of job going? Are there a lot of people out of work in Cabourg? I never see anyone at the job centre. Personally, I don't think that things have changed. We live just the same as before, eating the same rubbish as ever. '

A man carries on from where she left off. 'This story about a recession, isn't it something they've just made up to make fools of us?'

Another man, behind him, adds: 'The recession, the recession, they've been going on and on about this since forever. The factories have already closed down. They could at least invent a new word.'

All of a sudden, everyone in the room erupts. 'On TV, they keep on saying that things are getting worse and worse, and they look at us like they didn't give a bloody damn. They're strong and they put the wind up us. Aren't they going to take advantage of it to shove something even worse down our throats? New taxes perhaps?'

'You know, I don't believe there's a recession. I said so to my husband right at the start. He agrees with me.'

Ignoring the hubbub, the course leader hands out little booklets explaining how to write a résumé. Most of the people present leave without joining the class, since there's too much to read, and it's all written too small. Before long there are just two of us left, trying to compose draft résumés in our notebooks. When we've finished, we ask where we can type out and print the result. They haven't got any facilities.

As we leave, in the entrance hall I hear somebody saying, 'Calm down, just go and sit over there', but I don't even look round. I want to get outside.

I have one last job offer to check out, on a campsite in Blainville. I've decided to go straightaway to the cleaning company, L'Immaculée in Caen, which put the advert out.

Madame Fauveau interviews people in such a tiny office that it seems to open directly onto the pavement. Two women applicants are already explaining to her that they're ready to do anything, they're even available Sundays, with transferable skills. They must have been on the same course: I can see I'm off to a bad start. Behind a partition wall, three employees are totting up columns of figures without saying a word.

It's my turn. Madame Fauveau has a long, rather melancholy face, with blurred outlines, as if life has eroded it away. She reads out my résumé in an amazingly gentle voice. 'Can I ask why you haven't worked for several years?'

I tell her my story about having been with a garage owner.

'What income have you got? Unemployment benefit?'

'No, nothing.'

'Not even the minimum welfare?'

I stammer that I prefer not to. She raises her staring, thoughtful eyes and gazes at me. There is a job that might

suit me, a campsite, not the one in Blainville, but another
one called the White Horse, in a town near the Mother-of-
Pearl Coast. It would be a contract for three and a quarter
hours every Saturday morning, with a car share organized by
the company, in one of their own vans. She needs to talk to
the boss about me first: he's the only one who can give the
go-ahead. While we're talking, the phone rings and I hear
Madame Fauveau answer: 'It's already taken.' I have to come
back on Saturday for the campsite. I can't convince myself
it's going to work out.

As I'm leaving, Marilou's name flashes on the screen of my
mobile. Since we've both been working on the ferry, she's
been inundating me with heart-rending messages: 'Don't
forget me this evening. Come and get me.' 'Have you got
a clove of garlic to lend me?' 'Do you know where to get
charcoal for the barbecue?'

Marilou lives along the canal in Caen, in a modern building block. It's much too early, about 8.30 p.m., when I
ring her doorbell. To tell the truth, I'm in a hurry to get
to Ouistreham. She's having dinner with her boyfriend, in
the darkness, with all the lights switched off. They're worried that the local 'youngsters' will see light in the window
and cause problems for them. Marilou cautiously lifts a tiny
corner of the curtain. In the car park, a group of forty-
somethings, gathered round a car radio, are knocking back
cans of beer. She lowers her voice and asks me, 'Can you see
them?'

'Them? Youngsters? But they're a lot older than you!' I say.

'"Youngster" means "layabout",' says her boyfriend firmly.

He's started to count out some small change which he sorts into different piles in a tin container. She gazes at him, her eyes moist with love, and then pushes back her plate. Marilou's got tooth-ache. She's always got tooth-ache. In these cases, the dentist strikes her as the most dangerous of solutions. Too complicated, too painful, too expensive: in short, it all seems like a different world. She holds her cheek, and her annoyance makes her round face look even more child-like. 'Anyway, if a dentist gets too close to me, I belt him one.'

The other evening, on her way home from the ferry, she called SOS Médecins, and they gave her some tranquillizers to tide her over. She's waiting for all her teeth to go bad so she can have them out in hospital, under a general anaesthetic. 'That's what everybody does now.' She looks at me as if I'd just arrived from another planet. Her boyfriend's already had it done. You wake up after the operation, everything's been taken out without you even feeling a thing, you go home as quick as you can, you eat mashed foods for a month, then you order a complete set of dentures, paid for by social security. You don't ever have to bother again.

I've convinced Marilou to try the dentist anyway, one last time, to make me happy. She was right: finding one's really complicated. Only a few will accept patients on CMU,* the

* Couverture Maladie Universelle provides free healthcare for those without social security cover.

social security of the poor. One finally took her on. Two months' wait.

This evening, Marilou is looking at me over her full plate. 'Oh, didn't I tell you? The dentist called back. He's had a cancellation, he can fit me in in two days' time.' I promise I'll go with her, in the Tractor.

We're among the first to get to the quay at Ouistreham. Some girls have switched on some music on their mobiles, very loud. They hold their mobiles and come dancing forward, four or five of them in a row, across the huge car park where silvery lorries gleam.

In the distance, the white mass of ferry slowly approaches, hazy, unreal, gradually filling the whole horizon between the water and the fog. I feel as if I'd been waiting all day for this moment.

9

The White Horse

When Madame Fauveau calls me back, two days before I'm supposed to go to the White Horse, my heart skips a beat. We exchange a few polite remarks, and I wait for her to get to the point: my job at the campsite has been cancelled, inevitably. Otherwise, why would she phone me?

Her soothing, almost sorrowful voice, suddenly asks me: 'Could you come to the office tomorrow at 8.30 a.m? There's a morning slot vacant, as well as the campsite job, of course.' I don't know what to say. It's the day and the time when I'd promised Marilou that I'd go with her to the dentist's. It makes me ill. The silence drags on for ever. Madame Fauveau asks, gently but persistently, 'So it's okay?' I can sense that she's doing me a favour, though I can't make out exactly how or why. She continues, 'You ought to say yes, I reckon.' I realize that I don't have any choice and, above all, that there won't be any second chance.

So, outside the agency at 8.30 a.m., the three of us meet up: Madame Tourlaville and I are cleaners, both on probation, and Jean-Marie is going to supervise us. He's slipped into a pair of long grey overalls. His wrinkled, weatherbeaten little face is oddly topped by a thick head of hair that's still very brown. He tells us to get into a van, one side of which bears the words, 'L'Immaculée, in cleaning since 1943', and the other, 'L'Immaculée, divinely yours'. As he drives off, he places an extinguished Gitane on his lower lip and says, 'So I'm taking you to Deauville.' This is to be one of only two utterances he will make during the whole journey. The other one is a remark he passes at a building site where employees of L'Immaculée were supposed to have cleared up the day before. Jean-Marie takes a look without getting out of his van. His eyes narrow and he says, in exactly the same tone of voice as in his first remark, 'They've made a right bloody mess.'

We arrive outside a little apartment block, only recently built, on the outskirts of Deauville, stuck on a piece of waste-land that is itself squashed in between the railway line, the main road, and some future horse stables. Jean-Marie tells us that we'll need to sweep out fifteen or so flats before the owners move in.

Madame Tourlaville and I soon find ourselves on all fours behind him. He's pushing an electric brush that sprinkles jets of acid onto the broad slate tiles on the floor while we use knives to scrape away the stubborn stains left by the workers. While manoeuvring his engine, Jean-Marie glances at us regularly over his shoulder. Irritation makes his face shrink: it looks even smaller. He unplugs his machine, takes the knives out of our hands, and shows us exactly how badly we are doing it. As soon as he starts his brush off again, Madame Tourlaville grouches, 'If he knows better than us, he just needs to do it himself.' She's a short woman, firm-fleshed, her hair cut cleanly round a face whose freckles give her a young, rakish appearance.

Jean-Marie is getting more and more irritable. He keeps saying, 'The boss is coming. The boss is coming.' We've been scraping away for an hour when he finally appears. Jean-Marie stops the machine again and introduces us – we are still squatting on the floor. 'This is Monsieur Mathieu.' He replies, 'Ladies, don't get up, pleased to meet you.' He's a tall young man, tanned, affable in tone, wearing a light sports pullover, jangling the keys to his 4 × 4. At first glance, he looks like one of those managers whose photos regularly adorn financial magazines for senior employees. However, on close inspection, he's not as self-assured – indeed, there's something stiff and artificial about him. It's easy to guess that this world of cleaning staff hasn't always been the one he's worked in. We stop scraping to say hello, we look straight into each other's eyes, and the boss suddenly seems more ill at ease than we are, hunkered down on our knees. There's a moment's awkwardness, which he interrupts by saying, in a tone of command, 'Jean-Marie, look, you need to put more acid in.' The other rushes over to a can and sprays the tiles with a generous dose of foul-smelling liquid.

Later on, the boss gives me a lift home. L'Immaculée is well known in Caen – the firm has an excellent reputation. Five or six years ago, when the previous manager retired,

Monsieur Mathieu and his wife left Paris and came to live here. They were thirty, or not much older; she worked in sales, he worked in advertising. 'We just came on spec,' they like to tell the newspapers. Their ambition is to set up a big business, and they announce that they've already gone from a workforce of thirty or so to over a hundred and ten. 'In our field, if you're hardworking and strong-willed, you're sure of never being out of a job,' Madame Mathieu often declares. Monsieur Mathieu loves to quote the example of that highly placed woman – 'straight As!' – 'who works for us on the q.t., at the crack of dawn on a Saturday morning'. He suggested giving her a better contract. But she won't hear of it; in any case, she's got a sought-after job somewhere else. She just needs to do a few hours' cleaning to make ends meet – especially without anyone finding out. Monsieur Mathieu comes back to this story several times, then asks me, 'What about you, do you work for other employers too?' I mention Ouistreham. He almost chokes. 'But that's a real hole, they're a load of crooks.' He immediately moderates his tone. 'At least that's what everyone says. I don't really know anything about it.'

'Well, it suits me, at least for the time being.'

He looks at me as if I were off my head. 'How can you say that? I'm trying to do the complete opposite at L'Immaculée. I want people to be happy in my firm, treated with dignity and respect. It's a *sine qua non* for me.'

At L'Immaculée, Monsieur Mathieu looks after the supplies and, in particular, fishes for new customers. He talks about the White Horse with pride – it's the latest contract he has negotiated, and he implicitly suggests that he's pulled off quite a coup. 'You'll see, it's really quiet,' he says. 'You'll have a maximum of three hours there and your contract's for three and a quarter hours. The holidaymakers have to leave the bungalows clean if they want to get their deposits back. So they clean everywhere. Your work is just vacuuming up after them.' He smiles as he drives. 'Really quiet.'

On Saturday morning, at the White Horse, I see Madame Tourlaville again – she's on the team too. Two dragon women keep the council campsite going, both equally young – but the one's rather skinny and the other rather plump, the one's blond and the other dark. They immediately collar Madame Tourlaville, who came along last week for a probationary session as cleaner. The two dragons have drawn up a list of her mistakes and declaim it to the company at large, in the indignant tones of a prosecutor. 'You put two undersheets on the bed in bungalow 13. There was still dust on the sofa in bungalow 32. The microwave in bungalow 11 had stains on its glass door . . .' Monsieur Mathieu comes over to Madame Tourlaville. 'Are you the one who did number 32?'

Beneath the anger, her freckles suddenly seem fluorescent. 'No, it wasn't me.'

'Yes, it was you.'

Monsieur Mathieu turns to the dragons. 'Don't worry, we'll find out anyway: we've kept the records.' In a corner of the room, the baker who's come to deliver the bread can't take his eyes off Madame Tourlaville; he's shaking with silent laughter. He runs the shop where she comes to buy bread every morning. She wishes she could sink into the floor.

Monsieur Mathieu goes over the details. 'At 1.30 p.m., you must be finished. It's written into your contracts that the job lasts for three and a quarter hours and, whatever happens, you'll be paid for three and a quarter hours' worth of work, and not a minute more. Is that understood?' There are five of us employees, we all stare at the ground, except for Madame Tourlaville, who gazes at the wall right in front of her, wrapped in an outraged silence from which she will shortly emerge, uttering the single sentence, 'Did you see the way I was treated like a real bloody pig in front of everybody?'

Outside, it's started to rain, it's pouring down, with loud cracks of thunder. Our little team is feeling a little discouraged, to put it mildly.

Then Monsieur Mathieu asks us to gather round and, waving his hand like a magician, he conjures up a bundle of biros and plastic desk blotters. He also brings out some T-shirts, navy blue padded sleeveless waistcoats, with the logo of L'Immaculée, and some big yellow oilskins. Then he announces: 'This is all for you. Take your pick.' The faces of some of the girls suddenly appear transfigured. One feels the objects. 'Can I take some T-shirts, please?' They've all been designed for giants. Never mind. Monsieur Mathieu says yes. Before long, there's nothing left and it's as if all the storms in the world had abated at once, when faced with the prodigality of this missionary handing out glass beads.

Next to an area where holidaymakers are putting their

tents up, the White Horse has some thirty rustic bungalows, generally made of wood, a cross between trappers' log huts and cabins on board ship. Our job is to get them back into shape between two lets. Each of us is given four to check over, from the kitchen to the bedding.

While one or other woman is hard at work, a dragon will sometimes pop up. She makes us count, wash, and polish, one by one, the little spoons, the pots and pans, the coffee cups, all the household equipment that's been worn away by battalions of tourists, as if it were her own family silver. I dash from one job to the next, clumsily, always expecting some rebuke. 'Here, on the electric coffee maker, you can still see a brown stain.' 'There, behind the fridge, you need to give it another go.' To give the stainless steel sink its proper sheen, only white vinegar will produce really immaculate results. ('What? You don't have any in your equipment?'), the electric plates have to be scraped with a Brillo pad ('Make sure it's dry, don't wet it, that spoils everything. There you go: it's much cleaner, isn't it?'), the windows washed down with warm water ('Yes, just warm water, and then rubbed with a jersey cloth'). How can we possibly not know all this already? The gravity with which the dragons keep guard over the destinies of the White Horse and its council bungalows is heartbreaking – and this thought alone prevents me from strangling them on the spot.

It rapidly transpires that we'll never be able to stick to the schedule laid down by Monsieur Mathieu. Seeing a crisis brewing, he's scooted off at top speed to buy the supplies we need and comes back with an armful of boxes. He exults. 'Just look at all the stuff I've brought you! You'll see, it's going to go much better now.' We are now struggling from bungalow to bungalow, dragging our buckets, which get ever heavier with all the utensils we pile into them.

Meanwhile, Monsieur Mathieu has set off on his own tour of inspection, going the opposite way to the dragons. I'm intent on doing the washing up in number 6 when an exclamation suddenly rings out behind me. 'Hey there, what are you doing? Why are you doing all this washing-up? And the electric plates with a Brillo pad? It's just not possible. You'll never have time, Madame Aubenas. Come on, you need to go quicker.'

A dragon goes past just behind me. 'What about the shower head? And the mirror – not the one in the bathroom, the other one in the kitchen? And the legs of the chairs? And the blankets, have you given them a shake outside? Mind you get rid of the dog hairs!' I try to protest. 'Monsieur Mathieu's just told me . . .' The dragon is strict and in no mood to joke. We have to do EVERYTHING, it's written down in black and white in the contract that I signed with L'Immaculée. She can get it out and show us if we want. I go looking for Monsieur Mathieu. His 4 × 4 isn't in the car park. 'He's just headed off back to Caen. He had a lunch meeting,' says the other dragon.

It's already after 2.30 p.m. I and the other girls furtively cross paths between the bungalows. It's the best time. 'What do you do when a stove is completely falling apart and needs to look brand new?' asks the one. The other: 'I spend my holidays on a campsite, but it's a damn sight better than this, let me tell you. It's a place in Brittany with a swimming pool and a safari park inside. Not like here.' Then we're off again, charging in every direction, exhausted and distraught. After a moment, we stop rushing around. We don't even have the strength to exchange complicit glances – we're stunned, dazed by our own powerlessness and the certainty that we're going to get more and more behind schedule.

I spot Françoise, another colleague, near bungalow 21. She's set everything down in front of her, the white vinegar, the biological detergent, the Brillo pad, the washing-up liquid, the toilet disinfectant, the brooms, the floor cloths, the tea towels, the jersey rag, and a heap of other things I can't remember. She tranquilly gets out her packet of cigarettes as the rain falls, her hands making a sweeping gesture. I hear the wheel of the lighter clicking, I see the little flame struggling against the wind and the shower, and the tobacco which eventually catches. Françoise must have been a cowboy in a previous life. One of the dragons comes by on a bike and, still pedalling, shouts, 'The roll of toilet paper that rolled in front of the door – is that acceptable?' Françoise doesn't move, she keeps her gaze fixed on a trail of black clouds scudding along the horizon. She announces, 'I'm having a smoke, okay?' And, as if she were in paradise, with the whole of eternity ahead of her, she blows out a smoke ring above her head, with a bravado that we will forever envy her.

We just finish around 3.30 p.m. We haven't eaten since morning, we can't carry our buckets, we haven't even had time to get to the toilets, we can sense a wild, desperate rage rising within us. It's the only time we'll see the two dragons having a bit of a laugh. 'When Monsieur Mathieu said you'd have finished by 1.30 p.m., we knew you'd never manage.' Dark Dragon explains that she's usually the one who does the bungalows. I ask her how long she takes for each one. Dark Dragon puffs her cheeks out. She has no idea. It's not her problem. When she has to check over a bungalow, she goes there, locks herself in and, when it's all finished, turns the key in the lock one last time. She's never looked at her watch. 'All this about fixing a definite time is part of the way Monsieur Mathieu runs it, not us.' I can't help asking her what she'd do if she had to check everything over within a precise time frame. Dark Dragon looks me straight in the eyes. 'I'd tell them to do it themselves.'

On the way back in the van, Françoise and I silently rail against the situation, without daring to reveal what we're thinking. We still don't know each other well enough. Her husband has just phoned. He's worried because she's not back home yet. 'He told me, "If that's the way it is, you're stopping the contract with White Horse."'

She's glad that he worries about her, but all of a sudden she conceals the fact, putting on her gruff cowboy voice. 'I told him, "Hey, actually, when it comes to my job I make the decisions." Anyway, he already knows this. It's *my* career, after all.'

She drives the van with one hand, as if she'd been doing it all her life. We talk together, cautiously, in little phrases that eventually add up to a conversation. Françoise tells me that she'd finished working when she had her sons. 'Then I got fed up of being stuck at home, it's all right for the first five minutes. You need to get some fresh air, see a bit of the world.' She registered with Pôle Emploi just a few months ago. She started to do temporary replacement work in a factory, at night. She moved into cleaning, then picked up a first contract with L'Immaculée almost immediately. Many others followed. Now, she gets up at 4 a.m. and doesn't return home until 8 p.m. 'I'm not going to stay on the lowest rung of the ladder. I'm ambitious. I want to work my way up.'

When she gets home shortly, the children will ask her, 'How much money did you earn today, Mum?' They'd never seen her work before. She'll feel proud, and this will make her laugh. Her husband will have done everything, the cooking, the housework, and it will be done well, since they are both sticklers for cleanliness. He's off work with a sick note. First it was his hand, then his heart. Now he draws invalid benefit. He doesn't want it to last all his life – he's struggling to find a new job. 'It would be the worst thing that could happen to us, living off social security. If someone wants to work, they work.' We're driving down a road lined with slim trees that quiver under the rain and, within its misted windows, the van seems to have turned into a little confessional.

We take the wrong fork. We head off in the other direction, but still can't find the expressway to Caen. We're going round in circles. Françoise looks as if she's about to explode, her face is drawn and haggard. Her powerful arms twist the

steering wheel violently, the van bounces along. Her husband phones again. She yells 'I'm coming!' All of a sudden, I
can't hold back the words: 'Fuck the White Horse!' We burst
into mad cackles of laughter.

The next day, Madame Fauveau phones. I have the feeling
she's keeping an eye on me. There might be a job as a temp
in a pharmaceutical company at Hérouville-Saint-Clair, for
just one day, from 6 to 7.45 a.m. I say okay. Straightaway.

10

The Union

This morning I meet up with Victoria in the marché de la Guérinière, a market comprising a few stalls alongside the council flats, where there are dense piles of sand carrots,* roast young cockerels, and live whelks in tangles of seaweed. Victoria does not deign to glance at them. 'Much too dear, I'll go to Intermarché a bit later.' We come across people wearing slippers clutching their shopping bags, while others are sprucely arrayed for their expeditions into town.

Outside the post office, there is a winding queue that has gathered under a sky streaked with violet, heavy with a storm waiting to break. The allowances have to be paid out today or tomorrow. The first ones to emerge warn those who are waiting idly. 'At the counters they're saying that nothing's come in yet. No point in hanging around.' Nobody moves. 'Perhaps it'll have arrived by the time it's our turn,' somebody ventures. There are hesitations, some people wander away, only to resume their place in the queue. In the laundrette,

---

* *Carottes des sables*, found in Aquitaine and Les Landes.

mothers fight with a gang of kids for control of the plastic chairs lined up opposite the machines.

An organization that looks after social integration has set up a restaurant with a cheap menu devised by an experienced chef. The tables are decorated with candles, which are lit even at midday. Here you can rub shoulders with the artistic milieu of Caen, which has created something of a vogue for the spot, and with the local notables who come here to celebrate their promotion – bailiffs, postmasters, doctors' senior secretaries. However, the restaurant is laying off staff just like everywhere else, and the organization for social integration itself is in a financial quagmire.

Opposite, a shop allows you to surmise what La Guérinière must have been like in the sixties, at the time it was built, when those who lived in this district were the envy of all. It's a clothes shop where you can buy dark three-pleated skirts that come down to your knees, blouses in blended colours and synthetic materials, flowery dresses, cotton handkerchiefs, elastics, wool, and all sorts of socks.

Victoria suggests that I go with her to see Fanfan, who lives next door. They were politically active together, in the same union, for years.

Fanfan opens the door. Before embracing her, Victoria proceeds to a rigorous inspection. 'You've lost so much weight! It really suits you!' Fanfan utters a coquettish laugh. 'I know, it's because of my cancer.' Then Victoria notices the hairdo, gathered like foam round a brightly made-up face – Fanfan has fussed over it to keep up appearances rather than out of any coquetry. 'You're nicely done-up too, I have to say.' Since her last husband left, Fanfan has picked up a little car, her first one, a model without a licence, towards which she keeps turning an impassioned gaze over the balcony, saying, 'It's my latest love.' Fanfan long swore that she would never be able to do without a man. Now that she's living with a car, people pay her compliments, and tell her she's looking much better. Even her mood has changed. Fanfan herself can't get over it.

All at once, Victoria's eyes soften and become nostalgic. Taking a trip down memory lane, she asks: 'Do you remember when you wanted to kill one of your husbands?' He'd moved into a place opposite Fanfan's, with his girlfriend. She could see them from her window. There was an old rifle in the house. The policeman and Victoria arrived just in time. 'What do you expect? I'd got him under my skin,' says Fanfan, moved at the memory.

We've settled down on the sofa in the living room. Fanfan makes some coffee, and opens several packets of biscuits – and, above all, she's managed to find enough room to set it all down in the middle of the assortment of knickknacks decorated with fur or feathers or made of china that adorn the little tables whose legs end in gilded feet. She proffers me a plate. 'So you're a friend of Victoria, are you?' I say yes. 'A cleaner?' I say yes.

When they got to know each other, Victoria was in charge of maintaining a specialist office in Caen city centre, an old building, with parquet floors everywhere that were hell to polish. When they came in, the employees put on socks: they were at home here, it was where their whole career was made. Even the engineers treated Victoria properly. The day after Mitterrand's election, one of them had asked her very politely, 'So, are you pleased?'

'They were the *crème de la crème*,' says Fanfan with a little whistle.

At the time, she had been working in a hypermarket.

'At the check-out?' I ask.

Fanfan smiles wryly. 'Being a check-out girl has always been a cushy number. They have a throne, their own kingdom. In my times, they were already the aristocracy. These days, of course, they're even more prestigious. No, I kept the shelves clean – not bad at all, all things considered.' The first time Fanfan went on strike, she'd been the one who organized the action, with a few colleagues: they blocked the hypermarket entrance with trolleys in protest against having to work on holidays.

The idea of missing a single union meeting made Victoria feel ill. She did the craziest things to turn up – things that would have been judged severely by her family back in the village, such as paying people to look after her kids while she was getting politically active. She couldn't have cared less – the union was her life, it came before everything else, and she could see herself staying in it until the day she died.

Victoria and Fanfan had created the section of 'breadliners', those who just scraped a living, a category meant to bring together the growing mass of people whose jobs had gone – hypermarket employees, temporary workers, cleaners and subcontractors. It wasn't easy being a trade unionist – it was a man's world, organized around big local branches, with steelworkers, shipyard workers, postmen. When these men talked about themselves, they would proclaim, 'We're the bastions of the movement.' This said it all. The rest didn't count. On demonstrations, some of them were ashamed of being seen with check-out women from Continent, and women carrying mops. It was *their* strike, *their* march, *their* banner, *their* union.

At the meetings, the leaders also had a special language, made up of political culture and technical terms, that the breadliners were supposed to understand but didn't. They asked the leaders to explain things in simpler language. This bugged the leaders. 'Can't you see you're boring everyone shitless with your fucking stupid question?' Sometimes the lads would laugh derisively when the breadliners spoke up. Victoria had the impression she was not really part of their noble class struggle.

One of the worst moments in the breadliners' branch was writing the political leaflets. It always went the same way. The girls started to get down to it, then, after a while, a union official would come over and say, 'Not finished yet? We'd like to head off for a drink.' He'd come back a bit later. 'You're taking too long. I'll do it for you.' None of the leaders had the patience to listen to what they had to say, and you didn't have to probe very far before the men came out with their real opinion: women weren't up to it, they fatally lacked any real 'awareness of the struggle'. They ended up writing whatever they wanted on the leaflets and, the following day, the girls refused to hand them out. They were called 'assholes'. Basically, the lads couldn't take their 'old wives' tales' very seriously.

In Fanfan's living room, we open some more packets of biscuits and cakes, mainly chocolate wafers, our favourites. We have another cup of coffee. Photos of husbands and children are brought out. Victoria tells us that, in her home, family albums are less well organized than the union papers that fill a whole section of the bookshelves, in cardboard folders.

It must have been at the start of the eighties, at a meeting, of course, when Victoria was still presenting the point of view of the cleaning ladies. A friend interrupted her. 'I've noticed that activists never sweep the union premises out any more,' he said. 'We're looking for someone to do it. Why don't you do it, Victoria, a few hours per week? You'd be paid.'

A man is appointed to lead the branch of 'breadliners' – a real man of letters, with a string of diplomas to his name. 'We need an intellectual to act as a worthy representative for the union,' the officials say. 'After all, we can't really send a check-out girl or a cleaner to the meetings.' Victoria remembers the deeply uncomfortable sensation of being 'not up to it'. In the headquarters of the union, when she's doing the vacuuming, she sees the guys sitting on the newcomer's desk and discussing things with him for hours on end. Then they all go off for lunch together. Only later, when they return, do they show any concern. 'Oh, you didn't want to come with us, did you?'

At the hypermarket, the management discovered Fanfan and her little union branch. They eventually chucked her out one evening when she'd absent-mindedly gone home still wearing her uniform: she was accused of theft. The union didn't move a muscle to help her. Fanfan abandoned her political activities. Her farewell letter, dated April 1986, was three lines long: 'Since my dismissal, I have been given no moral support from the team. That is why I am resigning from my posts. I cannot see any reason for staying in a union where I have no place.'

There is a clatter of noise from the stairwell. It's some kids going downstairs in their rollerblades. 'Do you remember,' says Fanfan, 'when every evening, at a particular time, there'd be a "thump, thump", two bangs on the ceiling? It was a girl who worked at Moulinex coming home from work and chucking her high-heeled shoes on the floor.'

Shortly after Fanfan's resignation, at the end of the eighties, the senior union officials tell Victoria that there's no money left to finance her post. She's been chucked out too. That day, she sees them coming out of the room, laughing. They're laughing because the meeting is over, laughing because it's at last time for a cup of coffee, laughing because that's how life goes. She shouts at them, 'You're a load of shits!' They just don't get it. 'What's up with you? You're making a lot of fuss. We'll do everything properly and find you another job.'

She goes home – or rather, three comrades have to take her home.

A neighbour drops by for lunch, it's the time of day when you can get recipes off the TV. Victoria wants to show that everything's quite normal and starts to jot down the recipe, as if there were nothing wrong. Her recipe book still has a few incomprehensible words scribbled down in it, on a blank page. 'Add 300 g, 1 spoonful of egg, 8 whites . . .'

Her girl friends try to get her to see reason. 'Get some treatment, Victoria.' She can't see any reason why she should. 'I haven't done anything wrong. They're the ones that are ill.' A cousin advises her to call in a priest who's an exorcist – 'a real one, he's qualified, not a charlatan'. Victoria goes off to see him. A tall chap, young, very polite, greets her on the ground floor of a detached house. He says, 'Do you want to know something, Madam? I've had exactly the same kind of hassle as you. There's nothing we can do about it.'

Fanfan suddenly breaks in: 'Anyway, Victoria, you're looking good.' Victoria's just back from a holiday in Brittany, with a club for pensioners. On excursions like this, she always likes the time during the evening meal when people start asking each other, 'So what did you do?' At the top of her voice, Victoria announces, 'Cleaning lady.' She puts on her roguish expression. 'I know I get up their noses when I say that. I just love it.' Fanfan starts laughing too. 'What a bitch!' she says. She means it as a compliment. One of her sons, who also works in a hypermarket, has just signed a contract in which he agrees to work for more than thirty-five hours and waves goodbye to his transport bonus. Fanfan gave him a good telling-off. But it was no use. He kept saying, 'The boss told us, it's either that or the business goes under.' He's not thirty yet. He rushes round everywhere. He won't tell anyone how much he earns. He's afraid.

11

The Leaving Party

On the quay, all the conversations keep coming back to Laetitia. She's going to be chucked out. Even her mates say she went crazy on board, without any thought for the passengers. On the ferry, sooner or later, everything can be negotiated, and even forgiven, but not when it comes to the passengers. You have to move out of their way when they embark and disembark, and vanish when they approach along the gangways. None of this is ever made explicit, you just have to realize this is how it is, very quickly.

Laetitia has been called into the offices on the quai Charcot by Jeff, the big boss, but she swanks around with some bravado; she keeps saying that Jeff can't manage without her and is going to beg her to stay. Her eyes are glistening, she hops from one foot to another, darting her head this way and that like a bird. Everything about Laetitia makes you want to believe her, to imagine that things will turn out okay, that life is a carefree and joyous thing, and that she will still be paid even if she sometimes goes a bit crazy on the ferry.

Having said this, Laetitia has already found 'something

else'. A fast-food place in Blainville. Not a job, of course, nobody would credit this: these days, nobody finds work, they just find 'hours' here and there. For the last three years, Laetitia has been working on the ferry for twenty-five hours a week. At the fast-food place, she'll have thirty hours – almost a stroke of luck. That doesn't stop Laetitia from feeling sick in the stomach at the thought of leaving the ship.

For her departure, she's decided to organize a leaving party. It has to be said that this isn't a very common practice here in the harbour. 'You already need to have a certain level to allow yourself such a thing, it's a matter of class,' a colleague remarks. 'Personally, I've never seen one, but my cousin works at the town hall, and he told me.' The list of guests has been drawn up, with the numbers being remorselessly determined to balance out any jealousies, rivalries, and the claims of different clans. Everyone has promised to come, even those who aren't on duty that day, even the bosses, and even Mauricette, who has given advance warning, in the tone of voice she adopts on her bad days: 'Anyway, I've already told you, I only drink cider.' Some have already encountered Mauricette at weddings, and she didn't seem to have drunk the health of the newly weds exclusively in the juice of the apple . . . but nobody has taken it up with her. It was generally thought that her rank as cabin boss obliged her to a certain reserve. This sudden skill in matters of protocol has increased the respectful mistrust that surrounds her, and kindled the idea that Laetitia's party would definitely be a 'grand occasion'.

Now it's 8:15 p.m., just before the evening shift, in the bare little room at the end of the quay, behind the harbour station, where every day we wait for the coach to the ferry. The tattered fog drifts across the water, the air feels thick and damp, clinging greasily to our faces and piercing our marrow.

Outside, the old gals in anoraks are trying to peer in through the misted windows of the premises. They say, 'All those scumbags getting together! Just look at them: who do they think they are?' They swear that, even if anyone begged them to, they wouldn't join the meal, not for all the tea in China, thank you very much.

So, inside, there's nearly a dozen or so young girls, all friends of Laetitia, shivering in the latest fashions – too elegantly skimpy for the low temperature. Some of them haven't put on their work overalls, and instead keep them casually draped over their arms. They've sat down in order of importance, the most prominent on a few plastic chairs, arranged around the table like in a kitchen. The others remain standing behind them, swaying from one leg to the other. We're in the second row, with Marilou, who sniffs disapprovingly because she's had to leave Caen earlier than usual and this whole business really doesn't mean much to her. She sounds sulky as she hisses to me, on the way home, 'Once I've saved 1,000 euros, I'm going to buy myself a scooter just for me.' The only man here is little Germain, hesitating between glee at the opportunity for swanning around, and a sense of caution that advises him not to get noticed.

Laetitia spins round, intoxicated by the prestige of the

situation and her status as queen of the ball. On the formica table top she's set out at least a fortnight's pay (some of the women even say a month's pay) in whisky, vodka, coconut liqueur, apple juice (because, along the whole coast, vodka and apple juice is *the* trendy tipple), five varieties of crisps in their torn-open packets and, prominently displayed, Mauricette's cider, specially prepared for her personal use with a plastic cup next to it. Mauricette hasn't arrived yet.

We conscientiously knock back one plastic cup after another, filled to the brim, on principle. We burst out laughing a bit too loud, and a bit too often – that's what we're here for. The scumbags are planning to go straight to a disco, a bit later when they get off the ferry. 'Who's driving?' asks Laetitia. 'Who do you think?' says Mimi. She's the only one with a licence, she arrived at the harbour this evening in a grey saloon car, with smoked windows; nobody dares to ask her from whom she borrowed it. She pulls a face. 'It's fucking boring going to a disco without having a drink. What am I supposed to do if I drive? It'd be too dear to tank up at the bar.' It's decided that Mimi will drink in the car, out in the car park, when she gets there. The others will wait for her, then they'll all go together into the disco. When the sun rises, those who are also working the morning shift will move directly onto the ferry. They'll need to remember to pick up some chewing gum to disguise their breath. Mona trumpets, 'I never get tired going to a disco. I'm the opposite – I can stay psyched up. Once I stop, I drop.'

We laugh and drink some more. There's still a quarter

of an hour before the coach sets off for the ferry and there
haven't been any more guests pushing open the door: there's
still the same gang of us, ten, no more than that, in the yellow
neon light. 'There's loads of girls that haven't turned up,
right?' asks Annie in a low voice.

'They'll come,' says Mimi firmly, raising a single eyebrow.
As ever, she's the one who regulates the mood and tempo
of the ferry. Mimi stands at least a good two heads over us,
and everything about her grabs your attention: her long sil-
houette, her hair that changes colour every day, the way she
looks like a countess busy on her estate when she runs her
dusters along the gangways and leans her classical profile over
the basins of the *sanis*, with an air of great dignity. Mimi must
be the only one of us whom the passengers notice: they give
her a double take, beg her to pose with them for a souvenir
snapshot on the deck outside. On her mobile phone, Mimi
keeps a series of photos of herself in stunning outfits, ball-
room gowns or strapless dresses. She shows them off on the
evenings when she wants to make a splash – usually it's a new
boy, recently taken on, who doesn't know how to interpret
this stroke of good luck. This evening, it's little Germain,
who clucks with pleasure but doesn't dare really look at her;
sometimes he turns red, sometimes white, and he's more
embarrassed than if he was seeing her naked. Mimi comes
from a family in Ouistreham, her father is a deliveryman, and
I sometimes have the impression that she'd find it perfectly
natural for a helicopter to land, one fine evening, on our tiny
little quay to sweep her away far from here, to her real destiny

where none of us can follow her, not even in our dreams. Stupidly, one day I asked her whether she'd tried to get a job as a model and, even more stupidly, I persisted, 'Don't you think you could find something else?' Mimi gazed into the distance. Her subtly husky voice darkened a little more. She said, 'It's too late. I'm already twenty.'

Mauricette has just pushed open the door of the little room. In spite of the cold, the windows are dripping with condensation. The volume of the conversations is turned to maximum, the table is bristling with half-empty bottles, and in the middle the cider is prominently displayed, with her tumbler next to it. Mauricette sweeps the scene with grim and angry eyes, brimming with menace. Mimi is the only one who dares to burst out laughing. Mauricette looks daggers at her. 'Oh yes, just look at her, stupid great bitch having a laugh when she doesn't even know why.'

Maryline, a charming little boy *manqué*, blinks. A few weeks ago, she had a fight with Mauricette on the ferry, for a reason that she explained to me the other day, drawing on all her eloquence and without pausing for breath: 'I was doing the *sanis*, Mauricette came looking for me, she told me to get a move on, she called me a spastic, my father had just died, I'd had enough, I told her, "Come into the cabin, we'll sort this out between us," she came in, I smacked her in the face.' Jeff made everyone see him in his office on the quai Charcot, it all blew over. Nobody was punished.

The cider is opened, and Mauricette's plastic cup is handed to her. She doesn't even take her hands out of the pockets of her navy blue jacket, but rejects it with a jut of her chin. 'Go ahead, have fun. You'll be laughing on the other side of your faces when you get on the ferry a bit later. You'll see how hard it is, I'll make sure of that. And I don't want to finish any later just because you've been drinking: it's *Intimate Confessions* on the telly tonight.' The corner of his mouth turning up in a half-smile, little Germain retorts – and nobody can tell whether he's being cheeky or, on the contrary, just trying to calm things down – 'You just need to record it.'

'Ooh, poor clapped-out old Mauricette, she still watches stuff on TV! Nobody does that these days. Why don't you splash out on a p.c?' says Mimi.

Laetitia's face is glowing with alcohol and she's suddenly afraid that the situation is going to skid out of control. She puts on a faint, playful smile in an attempt to salvage her party. 'Why d'you say that, Mimi? Everyone needs a TV at home! Otherwise, what would we do when we have people round?'

'Anyway,' says Mauricette in a peremptory tone, 'I still live in the Middle Ages. You know, you're all creasing me up now.' The table is covered with crisp crumbs and, in spite of all our hard work, the bottles still contain enough to make at least two squads of cleaners drunk. When we go out, the girls who've stayed outside part in silence to let our sparse little gathering through. We realize, all at once, that many of the women who'd been invited preferred not to come in when they saw that none of the bosses was there; they'd suddenly hesitated, unsure how events would turn out, and the caution of some had held back the others. Wouldn't it look bad if they went to a party? Don't they risk losing their jobs? They have no idea; it's never happened before. Some try to mutter excuses to Laetitia, claiming that they weren't feeling too good, or that they'd arrived late. The old gals sneer when they see us stagger off through the night towards the coach, our faces aflame. Mauricette sits down next to the driver, and talks to another boss. 'In France, we need a sense of order. People need to be brought to heel.'

We climb on board. I've been given the public *sanis*, a task which consists of cleaning the toilets in the collective areas, the restaurants, bars, and decks. From deck to deck, from one set of toilets to the next, we drag along, as fast as we can, a monumental trolley on wheels, equipped with a tank of warm water, a mop, some floor cloths, dusters, and waste bins. We need to wash, as quickly as possible, the rows of toilets, from floor to ceiling.

This job is done in teams of two: this evening, I'm with Amanda. No sooner have we reached the first deck than she utters a little scream. 'Shit, my piercing's just burst, the one on my belly-button. It was my favourite, a little dolphin.' She wants to know what day it is and if I know how long it will take for our pay to come in. She's hungry. Before setting off, she'd eaten some pork with lentils, half a tin full. She's worried her brother will finish it by the time she gets home this evening. The two of them have stayed on alone in the family apartment since their parents' divorce. Their father pays for the roof over their head, but can't afford any more. Amanda thinks they've got 8 euros between them for the rest of the week. We talk in short bursts, broken up by our movements and by the sounds of our work, when one pulls the chain or the other turns on the water, punctuated by 'I didn't catch that,' or 'Say again,' or 'You should see the toilets I'm in, you can't imagine how disgusting they are, it's just everywhere.'

Sometimes, at weekends, Amanda's uncle asks her to help him in her pizzeria. She feels it's different there. 'I feel more at home.' Amanda is studying for the *bac*, specializing in sales – but she's not sure she'll see it through to the end of the year. 'In the morning, when I get to my lessons, it's a no-brainer: I just go to sleep.' Her brother's younger, still at school.

She asks where I worked before. I recite my story about the garage owner and pull the chain hard in two toilets, to fore-stall any more questions. Amanda has heard perfectly well. 'Don't take this the wrong way, but now you've ended up scrubbing down the loos in a ferry – a bit of a comedown, isn't it?'

Suddenly, from the tone of her voice, I realize I'd better shut up. In a mirror in the *sanis*, I've just spotted the reflection of one of the bosses. We start scrubbing, without uttering a word. The boss comes into the toilets of the snack bar where we're busy. He's one of the nicer ones.

'Okay, ladies? Getting on all right?'

'Yes, thanks.'

We need to get a move on so we can go and give a hand to the cabin team – they've fallen behind. We rush down. On the lower deck, the gangways are filled with feverish activity. Maryline is completely drunk; she wanders from cabin to cabin, laughing noisily, her laughter coming in fits and bursts, like a car that can't get started. Mauricette places her hand over her eyes. 'Get her out of here. Get her out. I don't want to see her. It'll all end in a crying match.' To calm Maryline down, they fetch her mother – she works on the ferry too. She arrives, shaking her fist but with a protective look in her eyes, playing up her anger as if in a farce. 'I'm going to belt you one now, Maryline, so stop it!' Then she turns to the others and says, in an exaggeratedly indignant tone: 'She's not my flesh and blood, that girl. Can't be. Just look at the way she behaves.'

In the narrow corridors, everybody has stopped bothering about giving way to others. Far from it; we deliberately barge into one another, trolley against trolley, body against body. The guests from the party flap around in chaos, surrounded by the old gals, who are grouching about having to work harder because of the 'drunken scumbags', but delighted that they can savour their revenge. I'm on all fours in a shower that has been more than usually laid waste by the previous passengers, when Mimi almost crushes me. 'You're out of luck this evening – you've ended up with all the lousy cabins.' Her mouth is gleaming with lipstick, as if drenched in an enemy's blood, and her lips are half parted in a fierce smile. A girl comes charging up to her. 'You're plastered this evening. Better not lay a finger on me.'

Another girl is trotting along after Mauricette, laying into her. 'Have you seen the cabins Miranda did? She's one of the new girls, she was at the leaving party, right? She's left loads of hair in the sink. Why don't you say something to her? You're supposed to train the new ones up, you've got to be harder on them. You need to show them who's boss. Once your back's turned, they don't give a shit about you. Go on, Mauricette. And have you seen the way Florence is dawdling? She really doesn't have the right rhythm.'

All of a sudden, the feverish atmosphere turns into a general rout. A siren sounds, like a tocsin. 'Time's up, the ferry's about to leave. We need to get off, fast!' We haven't finished the cabins, but we need to disembark anyway, even if it means leaving the work incomplete. Employees on board will finish it at the start of the crossing, the company risks incurring a hefty penalty. Everyone has packed up their things pell-mell, and grabbed their coats, and there's a mad dash to the gangway while the sirens continue to hoot. From time to time, a name is called out, to check that nobody's been left on board. It's okay, we're outside, breathless, panicky, with the same stinging feeling, a kind of shame at the idea that for days there's going to be talk of this evening when 'we didn't manage to finish'.

In the car park, the cars start up, their headlights switched off. The end of the shifts always resembles a general flight, as if we'd just done something wrong, but this evening it's even more true. Before we go on board the ferry, time drags, the conversations stretch out, from cigarette to cigarette. But here we hardly bother to shout a few goodbyes, among the revving cars, the horns, and the wheels that are being made to screech as loud as possible. Some race to get to the car park exit, behind the control booth. I'm getting ready to head off when I realize that the Tractor's had a puncture. I can't change a tyre and neither can Marilou. Our colleagues' cars speed past us into the night. I wave at them. Nobody stops. In the motionless Tractor, far from everything, we're sitting there on seats that are damp and sticky. Although it's not raining, the window wipers are needed.

Olivier's family estate car brakes level with us. The whole family works on the ferry, the father, the mother, the daughter. I feel cold on their behalf when I see them extracting themselves from their warm passenger seats and looking for a car jack in the boot. Olivier bangs his hands together to warm himself up. We get out in turn. They say, 'We're hardly going to leave you there just like that, are we?'

In the Tractor on the way back, Marilou asks me where she could find a seafood platter on special offer. She's seen one for 12.90 euros at Cora, but she doesn't know how to get it home by scooter. And what about trainers? What's the price of trainers? Hers are always split.

All at once, her voice sinks to a murmur. In the future, the distant future, when she's put enough aside, Marilou says that she's going to have her own house. Do I know how to go about buying a house? How much might it cost, for example? Where do you need to start? And then, she won't have cats any more, but dogs, definitely. 'And then. . .' Her voice sinks a little lower in the night, the streetlights along the express-way illuminate her podgy face in flashes. I see her short upper lip quivering, leaving her front teeth slightly exposed. She hesitates, as if worried that she has been incautious, disclosing desires and ambitions that suddenly seem excessive. And then . . . and then she's going to take a diploma to become a qualified teaching assistant at an infants' school. Yes, a diploma, and then she'll make it – not like the CAP.* Everyone agrees that she gets on well with kids, even one of her boyfriend's female cousins – despite quarrelling with this woman at her wedding. And she's going to have babies of her own, too. Then everything's going to be the way it should be. She says her eyes are so tired they sting, she'd like to sleep but can't get off. Every evening, she lies in bed next to her boyfriend and plays on the tiny screen of her mobile until day breaks. When I drop her off, she always asks me to leave her right outside her door, in case the 'young folks are messing around'. Through the darkness, the curtain in her flat rises and her boyfriend's face appears furtively in the gloom.

The next day, Marilou gives in her notice at the ferry. I'll never see her again.

At 5.30 a.m., the sun hasn't yet risen as I drive round the apartment blocks in Hérouville-Saint-Clair, looking for the laboratory which Madame Fauveau has sent me to as a temp. I just can't find the door, the numbers of the buildings aren't in any order, the blocks all look like dice thrown at random

* CAP = Certificat d'Aptitude Professionelle, a vocational training certificate obtained at high school.

onto the concrete slabs. Finally, I discover the right spot. It's 6.05 a.m. A feverish little girl, the picture of wounded inno-cence, wearing the same white coat as me, opens the door. Without a hello, she murmurs, in a very low voice, in the empty laboratory, 'You're late.' She stares at me with wide eyes imbued with reproach, fatigue, and fear – eyes that fill all of her startlingly white face, eyes unlit by any light. Her collar lies open to display a bare neck that gives off a damp odour of night and sheets. She says, 'My alarm didn't ring either, but I managed to get here at five to six.' She's dissat-isfied with everything I do and her deep, tragic sighs pierce through the noise of the vacuum. 'Haven't you polished the table?' 'Haven't you scraped the putty off the floor?' 'Haven't you wiped out the drawers?' 'Over there, pick up his papers.' 'What else have you forgotten?' At every minute, she tells me what time it is, followed by the same remark: 'We ought to have finished.'

It's 7.45 a.m. It's done. Wounded Innocence barely says goodbye to me and throws herself into a car that's drawn up in front of the door, where a young man is waiting for her. She opens the door and I hear her groaning softly, 'My love, my love, if only you knew what happened to me this morning with the temp, it was awful.'

12

The Barbecue Section

Philippe at first wanted to go to La Jardinerie, a huge garden
centre on the outskirts of Caen, which is apparently offering
'a fantastic range of carnivorous plants'. But the puncture
in the Tractor has put me in an unenviable situation. It all
starts to build up: I need to buy tyres, I'm useless at mechanical things, I'm still looking for other jobs, a worrying smell of
pipes and plumbing has invaded my bathroom.

I say, a little tersely, 'Whatever do you want us to go to a
garden centre for?'

Philippe is surprised. 'It'll be a day out. A way of getting
some fresh air. Don't you like the countryside?'

'Yes, I love it – but in that case why don't we go for a walk
in the woods or on the beach?'

Philippe doesn't get it. He grumbles. 'You're always thinking too much about your work, you never go out. You need to
get some relaxation, otherwise you won't be able to manage.
La Jardinerie is the ideal place to blow the cobwebs away: you
see loads of people, you can buy stuff. It's full of life. Plus, the
shop's open Sundays. You know, I've got lots of girl friends

who, ever since their divorce, wouldn't know what to do on Sundays if the hypermarkets were closed. Anyway, you need to really try and be a bit more patient.'

I start to protest that nobody gives a damn about Sunday as, in any case, it's Wednesday. We end up by compromising: a drive to Intermarché (or Carrefour, I can't remember). This suits Philippe, now that he doesn't have any means of transport. He also promises to change my tyres. He loves doing that.

I go to pick him up from his home, out towards Bayeux. He's wearing a diamond in his ear and pointed boots. As we pass in front of the Novotel, where we met at the jobs forum, Philippe asks me to pull up. He looks at the revolving door at the entry, then, suddenly ceremonious, warns me that he's got something to ask me.

'Do you mind if I drive?'

He looks at himself in the rear mirror, and runs his hands through his hair to smooth it back. Then he gravely puts on his seatbelt, turns the key, and tries the gears one by one, like a connoisseur. At the wheel, Philippe suddenly seems bigger, squarer, more sure of himself, as if he were readopting a previous identity. He remarks on the traffic and even his voice sounds fuller, you can guess at the old Philippe, when he was a man with a job, a car, and everything that goes with them.

He's arranged the time and place for our expedition, with the precision of the fisherman who knows all the right spots to catch fish. 'It's better to go there round 10.30 a.m. or after 4 p.m. There's no point otherwise. There's nobody there, it's

a real bore.' So as to feel completely comfortable, we've left
our coats in the boot of the Tractor and we swan around the
hypermarket, each of us behind a majestic trolley. We look at
everything. We lift everything up to examine it. We remark
on everything. Now and again, customers greet each other
with smiles and questions about the family, just like on some
village square on the day of the fair.

At every shelf display, Philippe has childhood memories.
When he was a boy, the shelf of comic books was where the
cleaning products are now. Here he bought his first satchel, his
first LP, his first after-shave, and even today he could give you
the price of all of these articles. When he sees the special offers,
'Barbecue Festival', Philippe can no longer restrain himself.
'Do you realize? For years, they've got us used to buying things
without counting our money, and now we're not supposed to
have any right to shop. We have to give it all up.'

He becomes even more worked up when he explains to
me that hypermarkets are the best places to pick people
up. 'Imagine, you see a girl you fancy. You follow her, discreetly. Just as she's taking something down off a shelf, you
stretch your arm out to take exactly the same thing at just
that moment. Sorted!' He mimes the scene with some packets of spicy sausages while continuing his explanations. 'Just
a passing confusion, the ice is broken, you can strike up a
conversation. You smile at each other: "Go ahead." – "No,
no, after you." And then, usually, if you're not a complete
idiot, you can get somewhere. You can also work out the
times when someone attractive tends to come in, and you

systematically make sure you're there at the right time. She'll almost always show up. Anyways, it's always worked for me.' Philippe runs his hand through his hair again. There's a little smile hovering on his lips, his pointed boots clatter on the tiles and his trolley screeches triumphantly.

At the car accessories shelf, he offers me a car jack, a special model for women. 'It's a present from me: I'd like you to think of me sometimes.'

Out in the car park, the loudspeakers are belting out 'It Gets My Goat', a song that had already been playing inside the hypermarket as we walked through it. In any case, you can hear it everywhere, it's the season's number one – the singer performs it with a noticeable, drawling German accent. Just then, we bump into one of Philippe's girl cousins. She asks whether we're together. I say no a bit too quickly – it doesn't seem very nice of me. Philippe shoots her a broad grin, and winks with his bad eye. 'Not yet,' he says. His cousin seems to think I'm damn lucky to have found him. She asks me if I've got a job.

'Cleaner. I'm looking for employers.'

'She's being modest,' says Philippe. 'She's already got one thing in Ouistreham on the ferry, and another thing on a campsite. That adds up to twelve clear hours per week.' I know what the cousin's going to say. And indeed she says it. 'Apparently, the ferry's a real nightmare – right?'

The cousin spent twenty years in a DIY shop before leaving. The boss was harassing her.

'It's bloody stupid, isn't it? I'd had to fall back on social security. I stayed on it for pretty much a year. My mother did an errand, now and again, for me and the children. I owed money to the gas. One weekend, we pretended we were heading off on our holidays, just to fool the neighbours. There was even one bloke who made me cry, the moron in the fairground who was recruiting receptionists on roller-blades.'

Sometimes she felt like chucking it all in, especially the day she thought she'd have to stop using her mobile. 'I said to myself, "Right, that's it. I'm on the streets."'

The cousin has started to hum 'It Gets My Goat', imitating the German accent and swaying her head from side to side. Philippe is polishing his boots with a Kleenex.

A family accosts me. The parents and the children are wearing the same short red jacket and each of them is pushing a trolley.

'Is it you we arranged to meet on the Internet to look after our pets over the summer holidays?'

The cousin says, 'No, it's me.'

We go off to buy some tyres; Philippe puts them on himself, he's dead set on showing me how. He screws and unscrews while I drink cans of soda.

When he's finished, he makes a suggestion. 'How about if I went back to the hypermarket to get a frozen pizza? A quality one? We could go and eat it at my place. It would be a nice end to the day, don't you think?' My phone rings. It's Madame Fauveau asking me to go over to L'Immaculée. Straightaway. I feel a little apprehensive: I don't feel I really shone, the day before, at the laboratory, and I'm worried that little Wounded Innocence won't have given me a very good report. Or else it's the White Horse campsite and its two dragons. I take Philippe and his shopping home as fast as I can; soon I am pushing open the door into Madame Fauveau's office.

On her face I can see that melancholy gentleness that I always seem to inspire in her. One of their cleaning women, who has a contract on two sites, for different businesses, has just decided to take a week's sick leave. 'It's just the thing for you,' says Madame Fauveau. 'You can be her replacement for the period. You can head off to the first company straightaway. The second starts tomorrow morning, from 6 to 8 a.m. You can do it, can't you?' She looks at me in that way she has, as if each time she were anxious that I would come out with the wrong answer and she would have to prompt me with the right one. I nod my head. She looks relieved. 'Do you want me to warn anyone at your place?' I shake my head. 'Monsieur Médard will drive you there.'

Monsieur Médard's car seems, like mine, to be coming back from an afternoon's shopping in a mall. He says, 'Don't look too closely, it's my second office.' Packs of mineral water occupy the rear seats, and the rest of the space is encumbered with various objects; it would be a matter of some delicacy to draw up a list, but it's easy to make out a varied range of dusters and sprays. Monsieur Médard tells me that L'Immaculée has developed a great deal over the last six months. 'We run an aggressive policy, and that's the right thing to do. Did you see how our boss managed to win the contract with the

White Horse campsite? Cleaning is one sector that's doing well. These days, you won't find a single secretary who's ready to give her own desk a dust-down.' He smiles. 'That's good news for us, but it's a dire situation.'

At L'Immaculée, Monsieur Médard manages some of the sites and the staff who work there. He's popular with everyone, he has the round, cordial kind of face that you often find on the monks who decorate boxes of camembert. He heaves a sigh. 'Women all want to do cleaning, it's the fashion, but they don't realize that it's not enough to want to do it to succeed. I keep telling the trainees, you need to be available very early in the morning, and very late in the evening, and still be able to cope with your husband and children. Most of them end up not being able to do the jobs we give them. They drop out very quickly. Believe it or not, but we find it difficult to recruit.'

His phone rings. One of the cleaning women is ill. He hangs up, with his broad, good-natured smile. 'It would be a wonderful life if cleaning women didn't fall ill.' His telephone rings again. Another cleaning woman is ill. This time, Monsieur Médard doesn't make any remark.

The company is in a new industrial estate, at the end of a tram line, with street names that nobody can ever remember and an urban setting in bright colours. The building is recent too, and yet the inside is like a range of offices that have been reconstructed for a film set in the 1950s. Monsieur Médard shows me the little cafeteria with pale yellow tiles, the offices, the cloakrooms with their metal lockers and lines of big washbasins in white porcelain, the stores, the post room with its array of wooden pigeonholes, the toilets, and the meeting room dominated by the eternal dust-covered screen.

Monsieur Médard whispers, 'You're really lucky here, you'll be nicely treated, the people are polite, it's not very dirty. Enjoy it. I couldn't say the same of all the sites.'

He explains how to get the trolley ready, fill the water tanks with water that's 'not too hot, otherwise it kills the detergent'. On Friday I'll need to push a cleaning machine round the stores. Am I able to manoeuvre it? I answer, 'Of course,' with the self-confident tone I was taught at Pôle Emploi. He tells me, 'Anyway, it's like riding a bike, once you've learned how to do it, you remember for the rest of your life.'

The first instructions concern the manager's office, and brook no dispensation: everything needs to be perfect. He's the one who signs and seals our contract. The rest of the instructions are recited pell-mell and I probably forget some of them. The baskets always need to be emptied, but you change the dustbin bags only in the last extremity, when they finally fall to pieces. 'We pay for them. We'd be ruined if new ones were put into each basket every day.' Then the telephone and everything on top of the table needs to be dusted, 'but above all, you mustn't move anything from its place. Never touch the computer: some people have been accused of causing terrible crashes. Don't risk it.' Finally – and this is one of the rules on which Monsieur Médard places special insistence – make sure the armchair is perfectly upright, bang in front of the workplace, so as to give anyone coming into the room the next day an impression of tidiness and cleanliness.

The previous cleaning company had ensured the job was done in two hours; L'Immaculée has stolen its market by shaving fifteen minutes off this. So I've got an hour and three quarters to do everything, all by myself. Monsieur Médard assures me that this is a good thing. 'The minute there are more than three people in a team, the problems start. Good luck.'

Some employees have left, others not. As a favour, the manager asks me, 'please, please', not to clean his desk. He twists and turns in the most incredible ways to avoid looking me in the eye. My working conditions consist essentially in making sure nobody notices me, while gauging the situations when nobody must notice me at all and those when I can be noticed just a little bit. Sitting at their desks, two people are absent-mindedly drinking coffee from a plastic cup. They now seem to belong to another universe from mine, made of different matter, hazy and distant, out of my reach.

The sleeves of my pullover are wet under my overalls, my hair is falling into my eyes and it sticks to my plastic gloves when I try to push it back. I'm too hot. I spend all my time looking at my watch, with the feeling that I'll never have enough time. I get away from work three quarters of an hour late.

The next morning, at 6 a.m., there are four of us in a huge, completely empty admin building. The people who use the premises by day haven't arrived and, basically, that makes it more comfortable. Here they're in the habit of leaving messages pretty much everywhere, written in angry block capitals, like an admonitory paper trail guiding my movements. 'We're out of toilet paper!' 'Please sweep under the furniture too!' 'I found this rubbish under my desk: needs vacuuming.' 'Yesterday this basket wasn't emptied.' 'For the second time, clean away the coffee stains.'

One of my colleagues is looking for extra cleaning hours in individual homes, and she asks me if I know any. The other day, her father went on strike for the first time in his life. He works in the car industry. 'He can *see* the recession.' She corrects herself straightaway. 'But what's really happening? Some people are saying that it was all started deliberately to allow companies to chuck people out whenever they want. If this happens, we're still being screwed, and it's all a pack of lies.'

At 8 a.m., everyone rushes off, because of their children, shouting, 'See you tomorrow!'

Monsieur Médard reminds me, even before I've started the car. Am I free right now? There are two hours' work, cleaning and sorting an apartment between two tenancies. I take this as a sign of gratitude. In the car, he starts to worry. 'This'll make a heavy day for you, Madame Aubenas. Don't you mind?'

We arrive at the apartment. The caretaker isn't there. He tries to phone her. Her number's no longer in service. We park in front of the caretaker's lodge and we wait. We can't really think of much to say, sitting there next to each other, our seatbelts on, while the windows gradually steam up. The clock on the dashboard silently moves on. Eventually, Monsieur Médard tells me that he lived near Falaise for a long time, before moving to Caen eighteen months ago, where L'Immaculée hired him. He rubs his fingertips together to signify money. 'I had no choice: the children needed to go to college.' One of his sons was unemployed, the one who'd been an assistant manager in mass distribution and had been earning such a good wage. 'They squeezed him like a lemon. He had to be available all the time and even that wasn't enough. They dangled carrots in front of his nose, a managerial post, they all wanted a piece of him. Actually, they said the same thing to everybody. Can you imagine it?' The windscreen is completely misted over, we can't even see the caretaker when she eventually arrives.

The workers have left paint stains throughout the empty apartment. I need to fetch hot water from the basement, the electricity isn't switched on. I suddenly feel exhausted, I can't find anywhere to sit down just for a minute, apart from the toilets. I'm hungry and thirsty. Two hours' work *in situ* are paid: I put in three, but I deliberately refrain from claiming for the third, any more than I did for working extra time in the offices yesterday evening.

I look at the sky: grey all over. I've completely lost track of what time it is.

13

Passions

'What's your passion?' asks Madame Astrid.

I wasn't expecting either the question or the way in which it was framed.

'What's your passion?' says Madame Astrid, again.

She stops staring at her computer and turns suddenly round to face me, as if she were expecting to catch me dozing on my seat. Her blond pony-tail whips through the air, good-naturedly. She's my social integration advisor.

It was Pôle Emploi that prescribed three months of 'mentoring' with her, with one meeting every fortnight. 'You need a hand to get going,' one of the women at Pôle Emploi had told me, the day I signed up. 'This person will help you look for work.' She'd then looked at me a little surreptitiously, anxious to see how I would react. There are people who don't like this kind of measure, for a variety of vague reasons, including weariness, mistrust, and bus timetables.

Actually, my meetings with Madame Astrid have always been enjoyable. I didn't immediately realize that she was part of a private bureau, a sub-contractor (she used the word 'provider') for Pôle Emploi, which doesn't have time to follow up certain files, such as special plans or persons considered to be 'unlikely to work'. This is my case. This places Madame Astrid and me in the same situation, and creates a bond between us: we both owe something to Pôle Emploi.

Her office is practically next to the Orne, I cross the bridge and I'm at her place. At the start, I used to wonder whether what I could see between those banks so severely hemmed in by concrete really was the water of a river, as it seemed so smooth and motionless, changing colour only when there was a storm. Apparently, that's what the Orne has always looked like ever since it was converted into a canal, when Caen was an industrial capital. I go past a shop selling electric bikes, then the red and yellow front of a Chinese restaurant. The private bureau is above – a flat that's been turned into an office.

In the waiting room, a few people are sitting, their bags placed on their knees, like at the doctor's, except that here you can look at computers and not just magazines. Madame Astrid comes to fetch me: 'Madame Aubenas?'

In general, our talks begin with an appropriate conversation on cleaning, which Madame Astrid conducts briskly, even with a certain zest.

'When you apply for jobs, Madame Aubenas, what do you write in the "motivation" slot?'

'Actually, Madame Astrid, that's just what I wanted to talk about. I never know what to put.'

'I know what you mean. It's true enough: how can you

define motivation in this field? Here, my colleagues tell me that they find it relaxing to do the housework on a Sunday. Personally, I'd rather settle on the sofa with a nice book.'

Her gaze wanders over the walls with their tired paintings, the glum windows, and the anaemic and sickly potted plants – Madame Astrid takes under her wing all the poorly vegetation that she comes across and nurses it in her personal hospital, i.e. the shelves of her office. Finally, she says, 'I ought to give this place a bit of a clean with a broom.' Before, the practice had employed a cleaner, but she'd been the first victim of the budgetary restrictions.

For today's session, Madame Astrid has asked me to show her my résumé. I take out the one I elaborately pieced together at the Pôle Emploi workshop; I've since pinned a photo to it. I'm rather proud of it. Madame Astrid shrugs. 'Hmph.' She immediately rediscovers her zest. 'We'll do it over again. You'll see: it'll be like having a new hairstyle.'

She sits down in front of her computer. Every so often she turns and gazes at me as a new idea springs to her mind, then she resumes typing away furiously.

'What's your passion, Madame Aubenas?'

I eventually reply, a little flatly, 'In your view, what kind of passion might be of interest to an employer recruiting a cleaner?'

Nothing discourages Madame Astrid, ever. 'Music, for example. Do you like music?'

I decide to tell the truth: 'I like swimming and reading.'

She stops typing and exclaims, 'Fancy that! Me too! What do you read?'

'Classic writers, nineteenth-century novels, especially French or Russian.'

She shakes her head. Her blond pony-tail bounces again. 'I can't stand those! School put me off them. I read contemporary works, at least an hour a day, and at least one book a week. My friends view me as an avid reader.'

I've got caught up in the game. I ask, 'So . . . who are your favourite authors?'

'There's one I really like better than anything. He can express exactly what I feel. He has words . . . I don't know how to put it . . . He's sensitive.'

I can no longer hold back: 'Who is it?'

She suddenly hesitates in a way I haven't seen before; she seems almost shy. 'Patrick Poivre d'Arvor.'*

She's already hard at work in front of the computer again, her white, fleshy arms flying over the keys. 'And how would you describe yourself, Madame Aubenas? What are your qualities?'

Yet again I'm stumped. She replies on my behalf, 'I think you're dynamic.' She types: 'Dynamic.' 'And you're communicative, you're a good team player.' She types, 'Good team player.'

The résumé she hands over to me is a work of art, with different columns and grey tone effects. Perfectly naturally, she

---

* A journalist, TV personality, and prolific author.

picks up the old résumé, and peremptorily feeds it into her paper shredder, which squats under her desk like a dog awaiting a sugar lump. Her colleagues envy her this machine; she bought it with her own money.

Another of our habits consists in going over all the job offers. She says, 'I'm so used to this that I know what to look for, it'll be quicker.' Madame Astrid forbids me from replying to certain ads. 'One hour's cleaning per week in a shop on the rue de Vaucelles? No way. It's downright insulting. You absolutely mustn't go.' When something strikes her as really interesting, she discreetly leaves the room to let me make the call. It doesn't often work out. The small ads are melting away before my eyes: there were a total of 200 in the Calvados a fortnight ago, 100 the week after, 75 today. The employers are pulling back, hesitating; they prefer to see how things turn out. It's the same in every sector: all frozen, waiting. Everywhere and for everyone, even in the private bureau. The bank won't give them credit when they ask for several weeks' extension just so they can pay off a few bills. Even though the private bureau has explained that these are contracts with Pôle Emploi, weighty, serious things, it's to no avail. They are even told that the State is the worst paymaster. Madame Astrid herself, who played a part in setting the structure up and enjoys job security, has just been refused a loan for a flat.

This morning, on the radio, she heard a politician prophesying revolution. He said that the French would be demonstrating in the streets before long. She opens her eyes wide. 'Revolution? That's rubbish. People are much too afraid. Anyway, it's not serious, Madame Aubenas. I believe in you. You'll see, you'll get through – no, more than that: you'll be a success. You're one of my best files.' To be perfectly honest, I'm less sure than she is.

On leaving, I call by at Pôle Emploi to bring my details up to date. It's quiet, and a sunbeam that nobody had expected is dancing away across one of the computers. 'You have rights, but also duties. You can be removed from the register,' the little film croons. In front of the screen, a job-seeker has dozed off, his head lying on the big file with all his papers in it.

Two men burst into the agency. 'Don't be scared, it's all been authorized by admin. We belong to an association against unemployment.' They're handing out leaflets. Most of the unemployed people here contrive to have their hands busy, so that they don't have to take the paper or refuse it. Some people ostentatiously put their hands behind their backs and shake their heads. Several are afraid they'll be frowned on if they seem to be taking part in any political activity.

Behind the open door of one office, a group of advisors observes the scene. One of them, who thought it was an attack, is dabbing her nose and wringing her handkerchief.

The Tractor is waiting for me out in the car park. It moves off – something that always seems a miracle to me – amid its odour of diesel with overtones of hot plastic, as sweet as cara-mel. The other day, on the ferry, one of the bosses handed instructions to attend a session of occupational medicine, pointing out: 'Those who don't go will be chucked out.' My appointment is for this afternoon, a clinic near the Riva Bella beach, opposite the municipal casino, amid shops of shell souvenirs and children eating crêpes smeared with Nutella. This is the Ouistreham that I don't know, far from our end of the quay. I can taste salt on my lips. The sky is full of kites.

When you get to the square, with the town behind you, there is one last row of buildings of various kinds: news-stands, car parks, riding schools, small workshops. The beach starts just behind, a stretch of completely flat sand, eating into the two sides of the horizon, without you being able to see to the end. Then there is the sea, vacant and alive.

Outside the casino, I can't see anything that looks like a clinic for occupational medicine. I look everywhere. I run this way and that. I retrace my steps. Eventually, I stop near a caravan that I have been trotting past in both directions for quite a while. I'd thought it was a fortune-teller's booth. I climb three steps to ask my way. There's a notice hanging next to the door: 'Occupational medicine'.

I knock. I wait. Eventually, a doctor in a white coat opens. He asks me my name and, without any other form of greeting, announces, 'I'm going to weigh you.' He seems utterly exhausted. I start to take my shoes off. When I get to my socks, he says, 'Don't worry. Stay like that.' I climb onto the scales, with my parka and my bag slung across my shoulders. In the caravan there is a semi-darkness in which I can make out nothing more than his wandering eyes, shifting restlessly, never gazing at anything directly. He waves vaguely at a height gauge, then gives up the idea.

'How tall are you?'

I pull up the sleeve of my parka to have my blood pressure taken, then there a few eye tests and one or two questions. I hold my chin in my hands, out of habit. He seems to come alive, for the first time. 'Is it the teeth? You've got tooth-ache, right?' It's all taken five minutes. He hands over my form. 'Okay to work.'

In the evening, on the ferry, everyone pulls my leg. 'What did you expect? That he was going to come and visit you?'

Corinne raises her eyes to the sky. 'It's not even worth bothering to change your undies when you go there.' Anyway, in her view, doctors are all the same – they cost a lot, you can't follow what they say, they're difficult to get hold of. You need to do loads of paperwork to get your money refunded. And then it takes ages to arrange an appointment! And you have the feeling the doctor doesn't really want to see you, because you don't have any money. The time before she says she stayed there for ten minutes, the doctor didn't tell her anything and, in the end, 'it still cost as much'. Anyway, are they really as good as all that? Guillaume Depardieu may have been a star, but look at what happened to him. Everyone agrees. Suzon wept when he died.* 'Those people are heroes.'

* The actor Guillaume Depardieu, son of Gérard Depardieu, died of pneumonia, aged thirty-seven, which he contracted while filming on location in Romania in 2008.

Blandine knows someone who had mad cow disease: she retails her anecdote with a face crumpled up with horror and delight. The others accuse her of boasting. Blandine shouts, 'I'm not lying!'

Suzon goes to the children's doctors – those ones, yes, they're good. But for yourself? These days she only goes to the emergency surgery at Caen. 'You have to take the car, you wait, but in the end it's more efficient. Everything's there at the same place, they examine you straightaway, there's no need to go back and you don't have to pay in advance.' She often says as much to her husband. 'You see, it's really good, like the hypermarket.' They could talk about this for hours, it's one of their favourite subjects of conversation.

It gets better. Catherine has come over, and Sylvie too. We huddle together, as we do every time the conversation turns to important matters. We've sat down on a small wall, and gusts of wind blow the glowing tips of our cigarettes onto our overalls. We have to extinguish them with vigorous taps.

Corinne says she's going to be 'touched'.

'Touched? Who by?' I ask.

'By a toucher, of course,' says Catherine impatiently.

He puts his hands on the spot where it hurts. You feel things, you get warm there, but sometimes you don't feel a thing. Sometimes you have to go back several times. Generally speaking, you eventually get cured.

Corinne looks at me sternly. She warns me, 'You shouldn't laugh, you have to believe'.

'Is it expensive?' I ask.

Corinne says, 'You have to pay. But it's not reimbursed on social security, of course.'

As the evening falls, the neon lights announce in green: 'Wind force 6 to 7.' As she speaks, Corinne rolls herself a cigarette; she puts very little tobacco in it, just a tiny pinch, then she arranges the cigarettes in an empty packet of Marlboros. Sidonie asks, 'Mind if I have one?' Corinne pulls a face and Sidonie implores her. 'Please, my husband never leaves any for me. You know what life with him is like . . .' Without uttering a word, Corinne passes the packet over to her. I've started to bring an apple with me, to keep my hands busy and make sure I don't start smoking again. Some other girls come up, curious to hear our whispering. 'What are you talking about?'

For eczema, it's better to go to the holy well at Dozulé. 'It works for scabs on the scalp too,' says Corinne. 'My husband's done it.' Otherwise, you can get treated for almost anything at Little Lourdes, at Hérouville-Saint-Clair. Along the canal, a replica of the sanctuary at Lourdes was built at the end of the nineteenth century, on the hollowed-out sides of a hill, with the basilica, the grotto, and the winding path of the pilgrimage route. It's not as big as the original, just two thirds the size. 'But it still works,' Annick assures us.

It was a wine seller from Rouen, Jules Dubosq, who had it built to thank the Virgin for his wife's miraculous recovery. 'He rejoiced to see pilgrims coming here whose modest income prevented them from going all the way to Lourdes,' says a plaque at the entry. From here, you can now see the washing hanging from the balcony of the council flats close by and, further away, the old industrial estate.

'Poor Virgin Mary,' says the custodian. 'If only you knew what people ask her for. And they come to see her when it's too late, always at the last minute, of course! They don't even know how to make a bouquet of flowers: look, they've squeezed the daisies too tightly together.'

14

The Gang of Morons

Françoise had warned us: 'The shit's going to fly on Tuesday at the White Horse campsite.' It's Tuesday, we're at the White Horse, and everything seems to suggest that Françoise was right, yet again.

A few days ago, a saleswoman from L'Immaculée telephoned me. 'This week, you're going to the White Horse on Tuesday and not Saturday, unlike what's stated in your contract.' I vaguely protest: 'But the two ladies at the campsite told us . . .'

She cuts me short. 'Never mind what they say. You don't have to agree with them, you're not being paid by the campsite. You are *our* employee. You need to obey *us*. Have you understood what I'm telling you?'

I reply that I'm not sure I'll be able to come on Tuesday. There's a long silence at the other end of the line. Then: 'You've got so many things to do, Madame Aubenas, that you can't come on Tuesday? Is that what you're trying to tell me? Have another think and phone me back as soon as you can.'

She hangs up. Out in the street, under the windows of the

apartment block, the smell of grilled meat wafts through the air. The fast-food place next door has just started cooking its steaks; it must be nearly noon. The mopeds of the local delivery men putter along. What if the saleswoman is going off to lunch? I call her back in a panic. 'It's fine, I'll come on Tuesday.'

'You gave me quite a surprise. I kept wandering, whatever's the matter with Madame Aubenas?'

I suddenly feel that I have just skirted the abyss. I have to sit down suddenly on the sofa – which also acts as my bed – while a violent cascade of water shakes the dividing wall at the end of my room, like a dike on the point of giving way under the onrush of a hurricane. To begin with, the rumble woke me with a start at night-time. Now it reassures me. It's the woman next door using the bathroom.

When I arrive at the campsite, Madame Tourlaville, my colleague, is already there. A dense fine rain whips and stings your face like a fistful of nettles. As we wait for the bungalows to be allocated, we talk business, seriously, tugging at our overalls. Madame Tourlaville's is too tight for her; mine hangs open on me.

Madame Tourlaville doesn't dare to ask how much we are going to be paid. She explains, 'You can understand, it wouldn't seem right. Who will they take me for?' Together with her son, who's at school and has the same freckles, she's totted it up: we work at least five hours every shift at the campsite – sometimes more – whereas our contract states that we get paid only for three and a quarter hours.

I remind her that Monsieur Mathieu, our boss, had told us on the first day that we wouldn't get a penny more, no overtime, whatever happens. Madame Tourlaville sighs that she had thought as much. 'I was hoping I hadn't heard right.' In any case, she's not going to protest. She's afraid she might lose everything. L'Immaculée has found two other contracts for her, five and a half hours per week to clean stairwells in a block of flats and one and three quarter hours per day in a croissant shop before it opens. The apartment block is near where she lives, but the croissant shop is nearly fourteen miles away. Given the cost of petrol, this second contract will bring her hardly any more in and she'll be spending as much time travelling as she does working.

'So you turned it down?' I ask her.

'No.'

She's hoping to get another contract, very soon, one with such good terms that it will make up for the sacrifices she's making both for the croissant shop and for the White Horse.

'Do you think they'll give it me? Perhaps it's all a lot of flannel.'

We tell each other that in any case you can't afford to turn a job down. 'If you refuse just once, you're screwed, wiped out, down the drain. They'll never phone you back. There are loads of people queuing up behind us. Do you remember how hard it was when we didn't have a thing?'

Madame Tourlaville's eyes make a very slight movement, though her face remains immobile. 'Watch out, they're looking at us.' I try to look out of the corner of my eye towards the entrance hall, but without turning my head too much: the two dragons are observing us through the bay window. All of a sudden, they strike me as being incredibly young. I hadn't actually imagined them as being any particular age. Their dedication to the running of the White Horse, and their inflexibility towards every man, beast, or thing capable of imperilling this mission, give them the pale mask and earnest gaze of those who have found their vocation.

Madame Tourlaville quickly stubs out the cigarette she's just lit. She murmurs, 'You see the blonde, on the right? She hasn't changed. We were at school together. They must be talking about us, saying "Just look at those two sluts, getting paid for doing sod all."' After each of our performances, the dragons send a fax to L'Immaculée, containing the ever-lengthening list of their recriminations: 'In bungalow no. 16, the tray in the fridge wasn't cleaned properly' or 'In no. 24, crumbs were left at the back of a drawer.'

'We need to get a move on. Let's go and get the equipment ready,' I say.

Big Melissa arrives. Two other girls come over to us – we don't know them and they smile shyly at us. The ones from the week before haven't come back. We don't know whether they handed in their notice or were sacked. And we don't ask. The few words we've just exchanged go round and round in my head: 'screwed, wiped out, down the drain'. Our eyes meet. On the other side of the bay window, the two dragons are still staring at us. Madame Tourlaville says, 'We're not

going to manage it again. Anyway, it's not possible to do the
work with these schedules.'

The road to the place where our equipment is stored is
covered by a fine brown mist. In front of some big collective sinks, lined up outside along a wall, a holidaymaker in
waterlogged slippers is scouring a cafetière. A family in swimming costumes is walking by under an umbrella and, from
a distance, we can hear the muffled noises of holiday – a
child tapping on a bucket and the crackling of a radio. The
rain is still falling when Monsieur Mathieu sails into view.
He's still as suntanned, neatly combed, and sporty-looking.
In the leaden morning light he seems even more at ease than
usual. We know that it is he who personally negotiated this
contract with the White Horse; he has boasted about it quite
often enough as the jobs are triumphantly handed out. The
way things are turning out must fill him with a degree of
bitterness. Just now he met the two dragons, which didn't
improve his temper. On his eyebrows, drops of sweat stand
out, which he impatiently, almost furiously, wipes away, as if
the downpour was also personally hostile to him.

He looks at us and we know it's not going to be pleasant.
And it isn't. He asks where the T-shirts and biros he handed
out to us last time have gone. Some of the girls haven't
brought them back. Monsieur Mathieu yells, 'I just don't
believe it! What a gang of morons! How can anyone possibly
be so stupid? You were supposed to bring everything back.'

We stand there frozen. He is even more unbending than
us. Nobody looks at anybody. Without uttering a word, he

hands out to each of us a big bag in which to put the dirty linen from the bungalows. I suggest that it would be better to have two. After all, before we take them to the laundry, we need to separate the sheets and pillowcases on the one side, and the undersheets on the other. It would save us time if we sorted them as we went along rather than right at the end.

'You're just getting one bag,' says Monsieur Mathieu curtly.

Why can't I just keep quiet? I can sense the imploring eyes of the girls fixed on me. I just can't help it. 'But I reckon that . . .'

Then Monsieur Mathieu explodes. 'Madame Aubenas, I could spend all morning explaining it to you, but there's no point. I'm not sure you're capable of understanding, so don't try and teach people things they don't need to learn. It's going to be the way I say, full stop.'

He turns on his heel.

Big Melissa is as red-faced as I am. She says, 'The other day, he told me, "Don't be such a total idiot."' She wished she could have come up with some rejoinder, but she couldn't think of anything, and it still makes her choke. 'In any case, I was afraid I might start to cry.' The last time, when she went home from the campsite, she had a fishing competition with her fiancé. They're a team, they're champions, it's their passion. She was a complete flop. Her boyfriend lost his temper. 'What the hell are you playing at?' She replied, 'My mind's still at the White Horse.' The other fishers started to tease them, at the end of the competition. 'So, you two lovers, when d'you think you're going to make some babies?' The fiancé laughed. 'Melissa? A child? She puts work before every-thing else.' Big Melissa says that it's true. She's an 'executive woman'.

We get our pails, while Françoise, who has just come from admin, divides out the lodges: there are nineteen altogether, plus four that need to be re-done, on the orders of the drag-ons. All of a sudden, it's her turn to fly into a rage, all by herself, while Monsieur Mathieu is already walking away over the closely mown lawn, we don't know where to. Françoise cocks her head, and scowls. 'He'd better not talk to me like that, it's dead and buried. It's a question of dignity.' She's just been appointed head of a team on the site and we look at her without knowing whether she is to be pitied or congratulated. It's precisely for this reason that she wanted the job: to prove that she can manage it, take a step up the ladder. When she picked up her pail, she rolled her round shoulders as if she was off to fight against the entire campsite with distilled vinegar and her green scourer.

Monsieur Mathieu reappears. 'What are you still waiting here for? That explains why you're always late.' The list of tasks has grown longer since last time. Now we also need to clean the windows, and air the covers of the sofa.

Big Melissa says, 'The harder he makes us work, the shittier we feel. The shittier we feel, the more we let ourselves get ground down'.

The other girls have finally hit their stride and are keep-ing to it, getting through the job with precise movements, so doughtily that there seem to be several of them per bungalow.

Not me. My morning is consumed in a panic-stricken frenzy, and I feel that I'm playing a game that I've already lost. One of the dragons has resumed her tours of inspection on her bike. 'There's some dog mess outside your bungalow. You need to pick it up.'

I'm aware that I'm not up to my job, but I'd like at least to see how the others manage. I decide to go into the bungalow where Madame Tourlaville is working and surprise her by imitating Monsieur Mathieu's loud voice: 'Hey, you moron, what a pigsty!' Madame Tourlaville jumps out of her skin, collapses onto a plastic chair clutching one of her breasts, and then springs to her feet, saying, 'Shit, I've just washed this one down,' and fans herself with her cloth. We decide to call ourselves 'the gang of morons' forever, though this doesn't really make us laugh. We're really edgy, we talk in low voices, and keep glancing towards the door, as if it was forbidden.

The state of Madame Tourlaville's bungalow is the last straw for me: it looks like an advert for detergents – it's so clean. I'll never manage to scrub a sink like her, let alone the rest. I try to work faster, and rub harder. It makes things worse.

Françoise had asked us to bring a snack lunch. We eat it standing up around the van, and take it in turns to sit down for a few moments on the front seat, where it's dry. We finish three hours late, and all walk the same way, stiff in the legs, with numb knees and two paralysed arms that weigh heavier than the pails.

It's pouring down on the road home, and the van seems to

be travelling under the waves of the sea. I wish it was true and that the van would never rise to the surface. I'm going to be chucked out, whatever happens. 'Screwed, wiped out, down the drain.'

Fortunately, Françoise keeps up a stream of chatter. She used to work in the restaurant business, with her husband. They changed with the seasons – summers on the coast, winters in the mountains. They'd pile a few clothes and an iron into the boot of the car, and a few cardboard boxes – not even a suitcase. They'd arrive somewhere, find a job that evening, and dance the night away. They hardly slept. 'There was money to be made in the restaurant trade, in those days.' Her story acts on me like a tranquillizer, and the music of her voice merges with the soft regular swish of the wheels on the wet road surface. I feel my head growing gradually emptier in the car's damp warmth.

Françoise and her husband stopped doing seasonal work when they had children. For her sons, she wants everything – she wants the best: fashionable clothes, braces for their teeth, holidays, a pet dog. Her husband is still on sick leave. Suddenly, I can't hear a single sound. Why isn't the story continuing? I don't want it to ever end. I reluctantly open one eye. Françoise's face is a few inches from mine and she's looking for her cigarettes. The van has stopped in the car park, next to the Tractor. We're back in Caen. She says, 'Will you be okay?' in her rough, reassuring, cowboy voice.

I clamber into the Tractor. It won't start. Nothing. Not a peep. There are days like that. I call the owners. Apparently this sometimes happens to it – it's a problem with the battery, which I don't really understand, but it needs two or three days to get it sorted. I try to phone little Germain – I travel to the ferry with him now, ever since Marilou cleared off. Germain's mother can lend us her Clio just to help us out. If it takes any longer, we've had it. I suddenly become aware of how fragile my way of life is, and feel that I'm at the mercy of everything and everybody.

I need to find something else just in case some problem suddenly brings everything crashing down to the ground. I've heard about a temping agency for difficult cases. It seems to me just the thing for the situation.

The agency is in a soulless street climbing up between La Guérinière and La Grâce de Dieu, always full of buses and cars.

We are received by Catherine Poiret, who has already written her name on the board and counts off each new arrival aloud as we enter the room. 'Twenty-four, twenty-five, twenty-six.' She calls out the number of the late arrival again, very loud. 'Twenty-six.' Then she stares at us reproachfully. 'It's a good thing we ask more than fifty people to come along – not even half of you have bothered to turn up. Anyway, a few will arrive late. It won't be their fault, of course. It'll be the bus, no doubt about it. And then nobody will apologize. Listen to me carefully, though in any case you'll forget everything. If you remember half of it, that'll be pretty good for starters. First thing: we've stopped saying that this agency does "social integration". We drop the word "integration" now. Everyone thinks that sounds too clinical. From now on, we need to use the word "solidarity". Got it?'

Just then the door opens and two young men, vaguely embarrassed, try to slip into the free seats without being noticed. The 'Good morning, gentlemen' of Catherine Poiret rings out like a pistol shot and hits them right in the middle of their manoeuvring. They both freeze. The one turns round, slowly, cautiously. 'It's not our fault, Miss, it was the bus.'

Catherine Poiret continues, 'In any case, all of you here, don't expect to find a full-time job. Even before the recession, things were tough. There's nothing left, including in the removal firms, except maybe in the period of evictions, and even then . . .'

The door opens again. A woman slides into the room, her eyes lowered. There's a silence, then a few chairs scraping.

'Don't you have something to tell us?' asked Catherine Poiret.

'It was the bus.'

We all expect a temper tantrum. Nothing happens, except for the ringing of a mobile phone, somewhere in a pocket. Nobody dares move. Catherine Poiret magnanimously resumes.

'If you register here and expect to be fed little beakfuls like a fledgeling, it won't work. You need to drop in here at least once a week. You need to be on time. You wait your turn in the entrance hall, and you behave properly. Don't drink alcohol in the morning. If you smell of it, I'll tell you so. I'm not judging you, but I prefer to say. You can tell me, "Yes, I've got a problem." In that case, I'll give you some telephone numbers. But you mustn't think I'm a fool. Some of you tell me, "It's my eau de toilette" or "I chew Nicorettes." Let me tell you frankly: sometimes, in the morning, when you come into my office, I feel like throwing up. A job-seeker who comes here, or turns up at his place of work, holding a beer, as happened just yesterday, destroys the credibility of all the others. You're there to work, full stop. You don't make yourselves a cup of coffee with other people's cafetières. You don't take a coke out of the fridge. You don't switch on the TV, including when there's cable. Even if the client has treated you like a dog, you don't raise your voice. You don't say anything to your employer. If you mess up three hundred hours' worth of work, I'll get onto your case and you won't forget. Get it? I'll call your advisor at Pôle Emploi and I won't hesitate to rubbish you.'

Some people stand up. They say, 'It's the bus.' I eventually leave too. In the entrance, one man is saying, 'You know, that Madame Poiret, she must have had a rough time of it all right. She looks really unhappy. I feel sorry for her.'

15

The Picnic

The place Foch, in Caen, has never looked like a real square. Massive blocks of apartments stand in a semi-circle around the war memorial, a column as high as the diving boards in the swimming stadium, on which a woman with golden wings seems to be raising her hands in preparation for the swallow dive. From this centre, several avenues radiate outwards, lined by blocks that were built after the war in the white, creamy stone of Caen, which looks strangely mouth-watering, like meringue. The square looks onto huge pasture lands, called the Prairie – old marshes in which, one stormy morning, I managed to sink halfway up my thighs. A rather rustic racetrack occupies part of it; here, depending on the time of day, you can see horses, crows, or men going round on a red sand track.

Today is a Saturday afternoon, and the place Foch must be the only deserted place in the town centre, which has, as ever, been invaded by families. You'd almost think that people were avoiding the place Foch: it's here that the unions have organized a new united demonstration against the recession, like that of 19 March that had swept across the whole of France. Half an hour before the procession is due to start, there is still nobody, or rather you can count the marchers precisely: there are six, no more, no less, with three banners and two vans.

I too go by without stopping: I'm meeting Sylvie and Olivier, colleagues from the ferry. They'd helped me out the day I got the puncture, and when they saw that the health of the Tractor was still fragile, they offered to introduce me to their neighbour, a Mozart-like virtuoso of the carburettor. The battery was recharged, but seems to empty spontaneously. Mozart agrees to take a look. When Sylvie informed me that she was expecting me today, I initially thought it was just a joke. I asked her, 'Aren't you going to the demonstration?' Sylvie must be the only person I've ever heard talking politics on the ferry. She shrugged and mentioned some vague trumpet rehearsal, with the town brass band at Blainville-sur-Orne.

Sylvie is a Communist. 'My father was one, and my husband is too.' Every 1 May, she sells bunches of lily of the valley for the Party. On the quay at Ouistreham, she regularly announces to all and sundry that she's going to stand for the union elections and fight against overtime that isn't always paid, or is paid only months later. The others always say the same thing: 'What's the use of that? The unions have been sounding off for years in Caen and the factories have kept on closing. Here, when there's a problem, we take it to Jeff, and it's sorted.' As regards the rest, the unions are considered, at best, to be closed shops, mainly useful for protecting their own members. At worst, they're called 'hot-blooded Reds', liable to riot without warning: all you can expect from them is blood and tears. In either case, the best thing is to stay away from them.

As a general rule, politics isn't a subject taken seriously on the ferry. On the day of the European elections, nobody, or almost nobody, was aware of the ballot. Fabienne had started to jeer at me when I tried to talk about it. 'Wake up, it's at least a year since Sarkozy got in.' Another remarked, as if automatically, 'That Ségolène should be hanged.'*

'No, it's not the presidential elections,' I said.

They look at me askance, suspiciously.

'So what is it?'

'The European elections.'

Fabienne shakes her head stubbornly, looking as if some smooth-tongued salesman was trying to flog her a collection of encyclopaedias in a foreign language. She keeps saying, 'Dunno', waving her hands in front of her as if to dismiss the topic of the conversation. 'We get taken in every time,' she says. 'We go off to vote for their things and in the end we just get bawled out. Le Pen – no good. The referendum – no good. Apparently, now, Sarkozy too, he's no good. In any case, we're always wrong, even when we win.'

'My father's going to vote, otherwise they look down on us

---

* Ségolène Royal is a Socialist politician who lost to Nicolas Sarkozy in her attempt to become President in 2007.

in the village,' says Martine. 'Especially as he's employed by the council. Personally, I couldn't care less.'

We move on to a much more exciting case – a woman in Lyon whose healthy breast was accidentally removed by a surgeon. This business has crept back into the conversation several times already, but today there are new details. 'Apparently, the health service is going to pay for her to have plastic surgery so she'll have her two breasts back,' says Fabienne.

Blandine is just about to launch into the tragic adventures of her sister's bladder, of which we already know several versions, but Fabienne interrupts: 'Does plastic surgery interest you, darling?' She holds out her hand towards Blandine to feel her low-cut dress; the latter gives a full-throated chuckle, and squirts jets of toilet detergent at her face.

Fabienne can no longer be stopped. 'And you remember the time you told me you'd never tasted the forbidden fruit?'

Blandine put her hand to her heart.

'I never said that!'

'Yes you did. You even continued to say it when you were pregnant.'

'No, I said, "I've never tasted that."'

Thereupon, one of the bosses arrives, my favourite, the one who has a slight lisp. Fabienne says, 'We were just talking politics.' The boss is amazed.

'Hey girls, not feeling well or something?'

*

I've just arrived at Sylvie's place in Blainville-sur-Orne, in a new district comprising little houses, all alike, stuck together like caterpillars, street after street. At the rear, they all open onto a little garden encircled by hedges, no bigger than a postage stamp cut out of the vastness of a meadow. 'Council housing,' says one neighbour with satisfaction.

I ring the doorbell of the Mozart of the carburettor. No reply. While we wait, Sylvie kindly insists that I have a cup of coffee in the dining room, in front of the cartoons broadcast by a giant TV. Now that I'm here, I give her a hand in preparing one of her specialities, tartiflette.* The most complicated point in the recipe consists in getting hold of ingredients 'at affordable prices'. A friend provides us with the potatoes, in thirty-pound bags, directly from the farm. We peel them. We cut the onions into thin strips, taken from a bag nearly as big but from another property, via a cousin this time. They are browned with pieces of diced bacon, extracted from a plastic bag, of the sort used in communal cooking, which Sylvie has taken out of the freezer. She adds different cheeses, harvested from various special offers at the shopping centre, and also frozen. This time, it's the mozzarella-gruyère flavour she goes for. 'You know, Florence, if we bought things the usual way, we could never eat like this,' says Sylvie.

At the far end of the table, Jessica, her youngest daughter, is bored the way you're always bored when you're fifteen. Horribly bored. Every so often, she goes round to see whether

---

* A potato and reblochon cheese dish from Savoie.

Mozart's back yet. Jessica's boyfriend is going to call by. They hear him parking his car. Jessica informs me, seriously, 'He's a docker in Le Havre, he's got a little car but no licence.' They both get in (the car is parked at the front of the house), while the children in the street run round them, dragging microscopic dogs along on immensely long leads.

Before she got married, Sylvie was a beautician. Some evenings, when she's in the mood, she turns up at the quay as if going out to a ball. Now she's on the Internet selling plants to help you slim, and working on the ferry. She's proud of this. 'These days, you're considered to be a social zero if you don't work, even by people you know. I don't mean everyone: the 250 euro rent is paid by my wages.' Mozart is still not there. I get back into the Tractor, praying that he's not going to stand me up. A pink mist has enveloped the sun, in a fresh spring sky.

I have to go and fetch Victoria: we're both going to a picnic for former Moulinex workers. Many of her girl friends work there, and Victoria had been tempted, at one time, to do assembly-line production. All the factories were recruiting in those days. She'd sought the advice of her union. 'When you were politically active, at that time, you always asked which company it would be better to get a job with for the struggle to be more effective. The organization would announce, "When you've decided, we'll tell you where to go."' In the sixties, when work on the shop floor was still a man's business, Moulinex was, in this region, one of the first factories for women – it was, indeed, a factory for young women. People heard about it far and wide, and flocked to it from all quarters. At Moulinex, the girls were very Moulinex, and real girls. They wore pink overalls and white socks, and they joined the company 'for ever'. Working there was a new identity card. It gave everyone a position in life and gave access to accommodation and credit.

In their youth, the Moulinex girls had started earning a pittance, but, in a world undermined by successive crises, their lot had eventually become enviable, almost at the top of the ladder, for unqualified labour at least. The girls themselves had gained in confidence, they had become ladies who grew old with their factory. Like those in the NMS – the Normandy Metallurgical Society– and Renault lorries, the Moulinex girls turned the town upside down when they went on strike.

Moulinex was one of the last big companies in Caen to close, after months of demonstrations, in 2001. Everything transferred to China, to general disbelief. Career guidance was made available on the site itself; Pôle Emploi – or rather, at that time, the National Employment Agency – had hired new agents merely to pay off the liquidation, and training companies realized that their fortunes were made.

Today's picnic takes place outside the railings of the disused factory. When you see the car park, you can imagine what the place was like when it was working at full capacity: a vast sea of concrete – 'at least two and a half shopping centres', says one former employee – where, today, kids are doing motorbike stunts. Ever since the closure, a group of ex-

Moulinex workers has continued to occupy a little building: a symbolic occupation, for which they are harassed by the town hall, which wants to get it back. This struggle to keep hold of a patch of the old factory is still enough to put a bit of iron into their souls. They cling to it with the same obstinacy as before, when they thought they'd be able to save their jobs. This was less than ten years ago, but it seems so distant – a civilization that's been swallowed up.

We eat sitting under white canopies, in our Sunday best. The starter to the picnic is a salad mayonnaise. A woman Socialist MP passes along the big tables, without sitting down at any of them, and a lawyer makes a speech on compensation for asbestos-related problems – a campaign he has just relaunched. The foliage of a tree casts a broad pattern of light and shade onto his face. We listen for a while, especially to begin with.

On the jobs market, in Caen, the Moulinex girls quickly acquired a formidable reputation. With the painful bravado of all losers – which is all too frequently viewed as haughtiness – they announce to all and sundry, to employers and bureaucrats: 'Watch out, I used to work for Moulinex.' They're called 'shit-spreaders', 'lazy cows', 'full-time boozers', and 'high-class tarts'.

The barbecue is served. Everyone thinks it's a great success (a few pain-in-the-necks add: 'for once'). I think of the comely Madame Astrid, in her office in the private bureau. During one of her interviews, she was talking to me in her direct tone of voice, as always, without passing any individual judgement, purely as a technician: 'Go to a demonstration? That's okay these days, it's not like it used to be. But if you openly declare that you belong to a union, or to certain revolutionary groups, you're finished. It's serious. Any employer who learns about it won't hire you.' Her blond pony-tail swung in the air. Most of the Pôle Emploi agents have recommended the Moulinex girls to conceal their past on their résumés, so as not to scare off the personnel managers.

Not many have managed to get jobs elsewhere, especially the young ones. Round the big table, everyone has another glass of wine. White or red? Everyone exchanges news of their children, their husbands, their dogs. We feel ourselves slipping slowly into a sweet and gentle haze of affection, like at a wedding.

Just then, the Moulinex girls launch out on their horror stories, their eyes imbued with a feudal and tender nostalgia for this work, where they all sweated away together on the assembly line. The shop floor was just the other side of the railings, a few yards away from the white canopies under which we are picnicking.

'The sweat used to trickle down our chins, we didn't put our glasses on because they got misted up straightaway, and we had those asbestos gloves.'

'It's easy to forget how much it hurt.'

'I did it all: the electric fryer, the microwave, the potato masher. It was a job for a beast, or for a bloke.'

They are now being advised to become temps for life, for 600 euros, or else to go in for the 'Job-service cheque' system, as they now call working for individuals (when the job is actually registered for tax). In general, their past means they turn such jobs down. One woman tried to become a cleaner. 'It was in a chateau, the lady would leave me the list of things to do, the windows, the stepladders, his lordship's shirts. They had to be free of any creases, she showed me how. There was no problem, they were nice people, they'd given me the keys, it was less hard work than at the factory. But I used to get there with a tight feeling here in my stomach. I told her. I couldn't do it: I went back on the dole.'

The Moulinex girls stick together. They no longer go for interviews in private bureaus. They've started counting their age like kids, in half-years, saying, 'I'm fifty-six and a half', to try to slip into government 'plans' that allow you to pick up a few bonuses and extra years of pension. They also kill themselves. There've been at least ten suicides among Moulinex girls since the company closed. The most recent was last year, she was fifty-two and a half. She left a note for all the others: 'I'm tired of doing shitty jobs'.

To get home, I go through Mondeville, an old industrial estate that's now become a row of supermarkets. Outside one of the last factories, Valeo, tens of white wooden crosses have been planted on the roundabout, like in military cemeteries – as many as the number of those who are going to lose their jobs. One poster informs us: '116 jobs have been cut, out of 580.' Somebody has scrawled, underneath, 'But the executives have been awarded a bonus of 6,800 euros.' The ex-Moulinex girls haven't been along to see them, as the different movements used to do as soon as any industrial action started. 'Previously, the unions made sure we kept in touch. Everything that happened was filtered by them, they had contacts in every place. There's nothing left now, we wouldn't even know who to go and see,' says one former Moulinex worker.

As I drive through Caen, the number of banners slung across the façades of the buildings suddenly attracts my attention: I count a good fifteen or so of them, between the university, the research laboratories, and the hospital. And yet everyone lives trapped within his or her own story, his or her own protest.

At Seaquist, which makes plastic stoppers, a tent has been set up at the entry. They've decided to call it 'the refugee camp'. In March, the management had assured employees they had nothing to worry about. In June, the first jobs were lost, fifty or so of them.

A worker serves out coffee in a thermos, watching the cars go by. He talks of being humiliated, abandoned. 'We wanted respect, we wanted to be heard – but without any violence, doing it all the proper way. The hierarchy didn't send anyone. The only thing they're interested in is that we don't smash things.' A few jobs at the company headquarters, nearly two hundred miles away, have been offered, but nobody dares go there. They'd need to sell their houses, change their lives, without being sure that they wouldn't be the next on the list to go. Nobody talks about the factory, and even less about the future. 'It hurts too much, I really believed in this life,' says one tall skinny chap. Under the tent, he fingers some old copies of *Ouest-France* lying there in a pile; they've been read and re-read so often that they're almost mouldering. 'So we may as well get the management to cough up.'

Some years ago, in metallurgy or at Moulinex, they'd all set off together, leaving their jobs in style in front of the assembled television reporters, and with a significant bonus. Others today manage to do the same, and the radio and TV networks talk about them. Under the tent, everyone speculates about the astronomical sums of money negotiated in this or that factory. Everyone replies together, 'It's more!' or 'It's less!' They shout each other down and get confused about the exact number of zeros: currencies start to dance round, euros, francs, and even centimes – millions of them come pouring down. Everyone thinks they have the one bright idea that could get them out of this mess. It's always the same idea: get the television channels to come. Enthusiasm drops. The television people haven't come and everything suggests that they'll never come to the refugee camp. 'We need to find some way of getting them here,' says someone, but everyone has already retreated into his or her own world of ghosts, endlessly mulling over equations in which credit, the car, and the children's education go round and round.

The tall skinny man gets up and goes out. He speaks to himself, under the insolent blue of the sky. 'Why is it the employees who are weeping and wailing over their factory? It's the bosses that ought to be sad.' His eyes are watering, but he says it's nothing to do with the situation, it just runs in the family. At Seaquist, when a request for severance pay was put in, the management replied that it wasn't as generous as the National Lottery.

Outside Intermarché, stockbreeders have dumped manure everywhere and organized a huge distribution of dairy products that they took down from the shelves in protest against agricultural tariffs. On the car park everyone is jostling, and looking for trolleys to pile the maximum amount of goods into them. Everyone's busy on their mobile phones: 'Get here quick, they're giving stuff away for free!'

There is talk of the workers who are also protesting and asking for severance pay. People envy them. They say as much. 'They've hit the jackpot. It's easy for them, there are so many of them. We get pushed out one by one, like pieces of shit.' The workers aren't very popular either, and everyone says so. 'The TV channels put them on all day long,' says a hypermarket employee grumpily. He's taken advantage of the confusion to nip out for a cigarette. 'Everyone's had them up to here. Even when they're unemployed, they think they're a cut above the rest. They think they're super-unemployed, they still keep negotiating measures so they always get more than the rest. The bosses have special plans for them.'

Piles of yoghurts soar from the trolleys, cartons of milk, a whole range of butters. The employee hesitates to take anything himself. He decides not to, and carries on moaning. One customer, a dark-haired woman who moves quickly and abruptly, tries to console him: 'Don't you worry, all those workers, they'll end up tumbling down the stairs, bump after bump. There won't be any nice cushion at the end of it all to break their fall. They'll land heavily like everyone else. They'll find out when it's too late.'

16

The Spider's Web

I go back home after my shift as a morning replacement. It's 8 a.m., daylight has not quite spread across the sky. My legs make me feel I've already worked a whole day, even though I've worked for only two hours. I've started to calculate my hours of sleep with the same precision as my working hours. I come home from the ferry at 11.30 p.m., I get up at 4.30 a.m. for the first cleaning shift. Sleeping has become an obsession. I park the Tractor and cross the road. At the tram stop, a pink and fresh-faced guy is making a deafeningly loud phone call. 'D'you remember the girl, a real blonde, we met at that disco, Le Margouillat, in Heurtevent? She's pregnant – with twins! And you know what? She says it's not me but my friend, David. I think that's bloody disgusting. I'm sure it's me. Anyway, I'm asking for a DNA test.' The sun has suddenly come out, it's already quite warm.

I open my door and fall into bed straightaway. I wish I could sleep. I can't. I float around in a vague half-conscious state. As soon as I really doze off, I'm awoken by pins and needles in my arms. I'm shivering all over; it's probably exhaustion, since the air is mild. My eyes are filled with sunlight even though I keep them shut. I ought to shake myself. But I can't, I feel as limp as when I have a temperature. I ought perhaps to eat something. I remember swallowing an entire baguette in the Tractor with a litre of Yop Coco, but I've forgotten whether it was yesterday evening, on my way back from the ferry, or this morning, on my way back from cleaning. I seem to be spending all my time driving, thinking without thinking, my head crisscrossed by complicated combinations of timetables, journeys, instructions. I must remember to switch off the alarm when I arrive at one particular place, take the exit on the expressway to get to another, put the keys to the building back in their hiding place, not forget to put the cafeteria bin out.

My first weeks as a temp are over, but fortunately L'Immaculée has added another one. 'The cleaning woman has gone off on sick leave yet again,' Monsieur Médard told me, with a jovial smile. This time, I have the impression it's for good. Two other cleaning companies have since given me contracts for a few days. They came to an abrupt end. In the first one, a girl working on the team chucked a bucket of water into my face. She thought it was my job to clean a glass door in the entrance hall of an apartment block. I maintained that I hadn't realized I was supposed to do it. 'Aren't you going to fight?' a colleague had asked me in surprise. I realized that the others had suddenly emerged – I don't know how – from the buildings all around. Men and woman had laid down their equipment and gathered round us. The one

opened a bar of chocolate, her foot placed on a plastic bin.
A guy brought his lawnmower to a halt. Our faces were all
swollen by the same impossible timetables, by jobs that were
simultaneously too much hard work and not enough. The air
crackled with overworked, aggressive exhaustion.

'I don't think she did it on purpose . . .' I said.

Then, as nobody moved, I added, 'Chucking a bucket at
me, I mean'.

There was a hesitation, then work resumed, little by little,
reluctantly. When they left, nobody said goodbye to me. I
wasn't surprised when the company didn't call me back.

In the second contract, I was the only one left when the
offices closed, in the administrative headquarters of a company. The employees left one by one while I started to clean.
For once, I had the impression that I was to some extent in
control of the situation: I could fill the water containers, put
the chairs in their proper places, polish the phones. There
was just one woman left in a collective workspace, a busy
little mouse, moving papers around in fits and starts, when
a man emerged from the room next door and made straight
for her. He whispered, 'At last we're alone!' His hands were
already on her shoulders while, in the same movement, her
body settled between the chair and the desk, as if spontaneously adopting a familiar position. She remained silent, but
he kept talking, in a dramatic monologue of which I could
hear only the music. I wasn't hidden – far from it, I was just a
few yards away from them, doing the hoovering and making
quite a noise. I endeavoured to make even more noise to

signal my presence, bumping into the furniture, banging the rubbish bins. They didn't hear me, didn't see me. For them, I was now nothing but a mere continuation of the vacuum cleaner, the same piece of mechanism, just decked out with overalls and plastic gloves. Eventually I left, saying clumsily, 'Sorry.' I thought of Victoria, sitting in her kitchen, a cup of coffee in front of her, with the eggs from her hens in the wire basket near the window. Victoria, gazing at me with her green eyes spangled with gold, her roguish eyes, saying, 'You'll see, you become invisible when you're a cleaner. You can't imagine how many things people have said or done in front of me, things I should never have known. Apart from that, I'm not giving you any advice: everything has changed so much that I myself wouldn't be able to work these days.'

I finished my work in the other rooms, before returning – discreetly, this time – to the main office. In the distance I spotted the little mouse from behind, in her bra. He was still wearing his jacket. I had to get to the ferry, I left without finishing the room. Did they complain? What about? Was I denounced for not finishing the work? Perhaps, quite simply, the cleaning company no longer needed me. No reason is ever given for hiring or firing you. When I phoned in for my pay, a secretary said to me, in surprise, 'Try-out periods here aren't paid. If we need you, we'll call you back.'

Today, a cinema in Mondeville is offering a cleaning job for between six and eight hours, with a rota for the weekends. Eventually, I get out of bed and make my way there. The

boss himself has been stupefied by the sudden influx of applicants – thirty people in a few hours. 'Don't bother to stay,
we'll choose from among those we've already heard from.'
He looks nice, and there's something cordial in his voice. I'd
have liked the job. I'm cross with myself for having screwed
up here. The weather is lovely.

I have to drop in at Sylvie's, for the Tractor again. This
time, the Mozart of the carburettor is at home. The other day,
he was there too, but he didn't hear me ring (he was watching
a horror film on DVD). His diagnosis? It's the gasket and the
carbons that need changing. I'm sent to get the pieces from
the scrapyard in Blainville-sur-Orne, otherwise it'll be too
expensive and take too long.

I drive down a completely straight road, as rectilinear as
the canal whose path it follows, and these two parallel ruler
lines, bordered with slender trees, as upright as candles, seem
to be the only clear and simple things to which the gaze
can cling in the landscape. Everything else resembles an
incomprehensible jumble, a moving territory of fallow fields,
waste land, collapsed structures, half-ruined buildings. Small
perpendicular roads lead to wide industrial spaces, quite
deserted, where the dust is twirling around in the sunshine
like golden sheaves, in the middle of skeletal little factories.
Grass spills up between the cracks in the concrete, bushes
and shrubs gnaw away at the buildings. Every so often, the
ghostly clamour of a factory rises into the air, a hoarse siren
blast, almost the cry of an animal, though you cannot make
out where it is coming from, or to whom it is calling, against

the motionless horizon. A man goes by, two men, sometimes a dozen or so, desperately tiny against the empty structures as huge as cathedrals. A lorry manoeuvres.

Some businesses are still active, others not, and you can't really tell the difference from outside. Between Caen and Ouistreham, the industrial estate of Blainville-sur-Orne used to be one of the most active.

All the life in the area seems to have concentrated in the scrapyard, located at the end of a road with a light coating of asphalt, near a railway line. It all looks like a scene from a Western. Two white plaster lions, life-sized, guard the entrance. Once you have passed this majestic welcome, you come into a hard-earth car park filled with more or less dissected cars, around which swarms a busy cloud of mechanics and customers. Some of them seem to spend all day there, coming and going amid the clatter of their tools. There is shouting, laughter, a hubbub of noises of sheet metal and engines. Behind, an employee is taking a siesta in a hut. This is where he lives, with a colleague.

Two young men greet each other, with contagious cheerfulness.

'Hey there, Tony, I didn't recognize you. Have you changed hairstyle?'

The other spits a set of dentures out into his hand. 'No, it's because I put my teeth in to go out.'

They can hardly remember when their 'old folks worked in the factories round here, good Lord, it seems so long ago'. They made car pieces or something like that, they can't remember, they were just kids. They wave their hands round the scrapyard and the stripped-down chassis. 'And now we're eating the left-overs.'

They laugh good-naturedly. France will end up like Brazil, they're sure of that; everyone will live on a pile of rubbish, trying to survive on what they can find.

Two gleaming sports cars advance at walking pace; the drivers wave to each other, as if they were stars.

I order my gasket, one piece for the car horn, and others for the carburettor. A littler gypsy girl disappears into the first storey of a shed, into what looks like a complete shambles of filth and grease, immersed in semi-darkness. To my great surprise, she returns two minutes later, bringing me exactly what I want.

Back to Sylvie's. When the neighbour lifts the hood of the Tractor, the children vanish and it's the men who come out of their houses to have a look at the theatre of operations. We have another cup of coffee at Sylvie's. Olivier, her husband, is busy on a building site. On holidays, he does casual labour in the restaurant trade. He's been a docker, a lorry driver, a labourer, a dustman. Often, the family all move together, father, mother, children, to do various jobs on weekdays, run the sound system for weddings on Saturdays, and work on the ferry in the evenings.

A child comes in and declares, 'It's done.'

'Everything working?' I ask.

'Of course!' the men reply in chorus.

Mozart turns down any payment for his work. Indeed,

Sylvie again insists on offering me another cup of coffee. I discreetly ask her if I should bring a bottle. She protests, 'Don't be daft! We've all stopped drinking here.'

I tell Mozart that the car will soon be due for its annual check. He replies, 'Do you know anyone?'

'No.'

'Oh dear,' says Mozart.

'Why?'

The chorus of men chuckle without replying.

In Ouistreham, on the ferry, Fanny is ill. Mimi too. When she isn't there, her shadow still hangs over the quay, people talk about her, discuss what she's done or will do. Apparently, a passenger has taken some more incredible photos of her. She's going to buy a BMW. Her brother's a hairdresser, he's the one who does her haircuts and shampoos. Little Germain is sulking. He thought he'd found a job as an assistant cook in a gastronomic restaurant in Troarn. He could see himself there already, as usual. He'd have left his mother's flat, bought himself a car and some decks. He'd have started to do the mixing, become a DJ. Actually, that's what he'd have liked to do. Or else an electrician – but he failed his vocational diploma last year, because of a teacher he called a 'carrot-top' because she hadn't shown him enough respect.

I promised him champagne if he got the job at Troarn. Young Germain just had time to cut his fingertip while peeling potatoes; the boss put him off the job only two days into it. He's going to try to do some proper training: it means you start off working for very little, but after that 'it's a permanent contract for life'.

Time drags on, from one desultory phrase to the next, on the quay shining yellow in the sunshine. It smells of summer. Last year, young Germain had been a temp in a service station. There were twenty youngsters there. 'It was incredible, we all had such a laugh, it didn't feel like work at all.' The year before, he'd gone to the Côte d'Azur to stay on a campsite with his parents, who hadn't divorced yet. They'd eaten mussels and chips in a restaurant on the beach, among the rocks. Can anyone know when they're happy? Young Germain had been happy that day, he'd have bet his life on it. The sea was so close that you just had to lower your hand to touch it.

One old gal started a rumour about another: she swears that she caught her having a drink with an Englishman in the Bar des Passagers, in the harbour station. The victim wept. A third woman sprang to her defence and insulted the liar on the Internet. It ended in a general fight on Facebook, where everyone issued threats to everyone else, saying that they were going to bring an action for 'harassment', before quarrelling about the definition of the word 'harassment'. The dispute shifts to the quay, and two clans are soon facing each other, siding with one or other woman. People push each other about a bit, not much, without any real enthusiasm.

All of a sudden, someone says, with assumed detachment, 'By the way, did you receive it too?'

And everyone comes to life: the harassment is forgotten, and the bar, the drink, and the Englishman. Everyone leans forward, even the men, discussing it in low tones, as if involved in some seething conspiracy.

'I didn't dare mention it.'

'Me neither. Maybe it's a mistake.'

'When I saw it in my account, I almost fainted. The payment was made directly, without a word of explanation. They didn't even advertise it on the TV.'

'I called my cousin, she works in the town hall, she didn't know anything.'

I have learned on the ferry not to try to join in conversations. It's not done; such an attitude is harshly judged. You need to be invited to chat – you can't just count on being there to be authorized to ask questions, give your opinion, or noisily voice your agreement. Even when you don't understand anything, you have to wait, to grab onto a few words, to let yourself be carried along by the phrases. Sometimes you can sigh, or even clear your throat, and gradually advance on the crest of a chuckle, thereby succeeding in gaining admission and obtaining a spot for yourself in the to-and-fro of the argument. I've got no idea what people are talking about, but I have rarely seen people getting so heated. Still, I'm thoroughly convinced I'd better keep silent.

'My husband asked at the butcher's. Apparently it's perfectly normal. All the families that get "schoolbag allowance" at the start of the new school year are entitled to the other allowance too. A social worker said it's an additional bonus, it's new this year.'

'I got 150 euros.'

Everyone shouts, 'Me too!'

'I'm scared of spending the money. What if they ask me to give it back?'

'You can go ahead, I promise you. It's allowed.'

At this point I venture in. 'Who's handed out this money?'

Different answers fly from all sides: Sarkozy, the mayor, Social Security, the government, Father Christmas, the benefit office, the ferry.

Eventually, everyone decides they really don't know, 'but 150 euros is a nice load of dough to suddenly drop into our hands'.

'Yes, it's our golden parachute. We're entitled to it too.'

The coach arrives. Everyone surreptitiously looks to see who's sitting next to whom. Some of the women have already caught a tan. I work out that from now on, the only current contracts I've got are the ferry and the campsite. And even then, I still haven't heard from the White Horse and I'd be surprised if there was any good news.

On the afternoon of the next day, I don't feel quite so stiff. Two days later, I miss my stiffness. I still haven't found anything new. I'm eating a container of Chinese rice that I bought opposite the station – it's not very comfortable cooking at home, because of the lack of ventilation. I know how it's all going to end: I'm going to have to go back to Pôle Emploi and do the rounds of the cleaning firms again. My phone rings. I hear the gentle, insistent voice of Madame Fauveau. It seems like the voice of an angel: 'Are you free? Right now?' Another cleaner is off sick. I want to say something to her, to tell her that – yet again – she's saving me from the edge of the abyss. I stammer, 'I know what you're doing for me. I'd like to say thank you.' She does not reply, as if I was clumsily upsetting some subtle mechanism that I don't understand. I'm scared she'll change her mind and hang up, that the delicate thread of our relationship will break. I'd like to say, 'No, please, stay on the line,' and I quickly fall silent in turn. Eventually, Madame Fauveau continues, in the same tone of voice, 'The shift runs from 6 to 8 p.m., working for a company in the lorry drivers' zone past Mondeville.' I'll find it easily. When I first came to Caen and was struggling to find accommodation, I was given an address as a last resort, a place where I could rent furnished rooms: cheap hotels, on the edge of the ring road, where the hauliers sometimes spend the night when they don't want to go right into town. The transport company where I'm going to work is situated nearby.

I stop off to have a cup of coffee in one of these hotels. Strangers are walking along the expressways with plastic bags dangling in bundles from their fingertips. At the windows of the hotel rooms, washing is hanging out to dry, next to the little satellite dishes and, sometimes, enormous saucepans. One man is explaining to another that you get a meal when you work for certain oyster farmers. 'No money at all?' the other man asks.

'No, just the meal, but it's a hot meal.'

The definition of my work in the new business is the same as everywhere else: I have to clean the offices. On the other hand, when I actually see the premises, I'm shocked. Everything's filthy, incredibly filthy. The post room and switchboard are filthy and covered with dust, the administrative offices are filthy, even the trolley I am obliged to use is filthy; the cans of detergent are filthy, the cleaning cloths are filthy, the mops are filthy.

In the yard, a small space is reserved for drivers doing the roads, with a cloakroom, a cafeteria, and a shower. Here, from the floor to the ceiling, a thick, sticky layer of brown muck covers everything equally, from the coffee machine to the door handle. 'It looks like it's been raining shit, doesn't it?' as a warehouse worker puts it, magisterially.

And yet everyone is busy at their posts as if there was nothing wrong; the head clerk is filling out his invoices in the middle of stains, the drivers are drinking espressos from cups that have lost their colour, the secretary is typing at a computer that's flecked like a windscreen.

When I arrived, nobody said hello to me, apart from one fat guy with tiny eyes, who looks like he's almost in charge. As I start to work, I can hear a susurrus of whispers all around me, people carefully moving around, cautiously trying to approach me. After a while, some of them are emboldened to ask, 'Are you the one that's replacing the cleaner?' Then: 'Don't you think it's disgusting here?' Some of them are more direct: 'Look at her, for example: she's not clean. You can see. Even her clothes smell bad.' A young blonde turns out to be the most assiduous of the official mourners. She keeps harping on her theme, in a tone of voice that is simultaneously whiny and authoritative. 'We'd like that woman to leave. You need to demand that your company gets rid of her.'

This replacement job strikes me as one possible way of redeeming my reputation, which has been at a nadir since the White Horse. I'm going to give some places a thorough clean to show my good will. I decide to start with the most revolting place, the drivers' shower.

The next day, I deliberately turn up an hour earlier. Still nobody says hello, apart from the same fat guy with little eyes. I respond by flashing engaging smiles at him, hoping to make of him an ally. I need an interminable amount of time to carry buckets of scalding water and try to scour away the dirt, encrusted in layers in the little bathroom. I lose feeling in my hands, I can't even manage to hold a sponge. I ought to be moving my arms, but they remain tense and rigid, as if they no longer belonged to me. The young blonde has started to hover round me. I can hear her talking through the squeaking of my mop across the tiles. 'You know, that other person you're replacing? Once I timed her: she spent just six minutes cleaning the toilets. Not a minute longer. She doesn't do a thing.'

The following day, the shower is dirty, almost as bad as before. Black traces of shoes mark the white rim of the shower as if someone had taken a shower while still wearing boots. Green plants have been left there; they disgorge a foaming torrent of mud, in which used rolls of toilet paper bob around. The fat guy with little eyes comes over with a smile. He triumphantly announces, 'I've just walked over the bit you cleaned with the floor cloth. Sorry, I've got it all dirty.' He sits down at the table I've just wiped, and dunks his biscuit in his cup of coffee. Crumbs scatter everywhere. He spills some coffee on them. He leaves the biscuit in the puddle and goes off, saying, 'Good luck.' I'm not sure that he's done it on purpose – actually, I think he's less mean than the others.

All around me, the rustling has resumed. And the sighing. Up comes the same young woman with the whiny voice; now she's pinching her lips. 'I like it to smell clean, but you'd need to give it plenty of elbow grease to get rid of all the muck. We're hoping for great things from you working here. By the way, what's happened to your colleague? I hope we never see her again.'

In the offices, I realize that little booby traps have been set up for me everywhere: bits of paper have been strewn under the table to see if I'm sweeping there; I suddenly have to give a room a complete makeover before I leave; tins of paint have again been left in the shower (some of them have fallen over). The rooms hum with whispers and laughter, which stop the minute I come in: all eyes are focused on every movement I make. Even the fat guy has stopped saying hello to me. I feel as if caught in a spider's web. I start to keep an eye on them in turn, coughing and looking at my watch with disapproval when two employees start to tell each other about their weekend.

When did the elements finally win? Does the other woman, the one I'm replacing, remember the day when she gave up, and allowed herself to be drowned by the muck and by her despair?

In another workplace, I happened to meet some of her colleagues. With them, she initially worked well. They told me she had started to walk more and more slowly. She had pains in her spine. And in her shoulders. She told them, 'At the drivers' place it's really hard. You have to scrub, and scrub, and scrub, and scrub. They're all on my back.' One day she phoned up: 'I've gone to bed.' Nobody ever heard anything else from her.

17

The Job Train

This time, I'm not going to miss out on my opportunity. A cleaning firm has selected my application, and I'm actually one of the fifteen finalists out of seventy-five applicants. 'You've got a good chance,' said one secretary, asking me to go in. I'm counting on it. Apart from the ferry, my situation is still entirely dependent on L'Immaculée, where you can never be sure of anything.

I prepare for the interview by repeating the formulae of Pôle Emploi, at home, while the cats walk along the roof opposite. They always end up by plopping down at the same spot, a tiny puddle of sunshine between two chimneys. There's a ring at the door. A family in the flat next door are asking me to help them plug in the printer of their computer. In the living room, the children are playing, phoning each other on mobiles. The older one is eleven. It's his third telephone, he takes good care of it, his parents are proud. There's a smell of coffee and crêpes in the house; they're unwrapping a parcel from the Food Bank. 'At first, we didn't dare to go there, but we're entitled. They're kind.' The father heads off to work. He's a house painter.

White Storm, the company that's interviewing me, is in Louvigny, one of the little towns on the edge of Caen whose population has exploded. Like all the others, it has its commercial area, a shopping mall built in a box around the hypermarket, a new, bright district, and, finally, the old village with the church at the end of a white road, behind thick walls, surrounded by an agricultural area. But this town is not as austerely tranquil as its neighbours. It's swept by breezes from the contemporary world: the grocer's is organic, the companies work in hi-tech, and even the shelves of the Intermarché have an up-to-the-minute feel.

The boss of White Storm, Barbara Netti, sees applicants in her own office, a simple white room, albeit with a certain sophistication in the details. She speaks first, and talks about this desire that had been gnawing at her for a long time: she wanted her company, her own company. Before that, she'd been an executive in the branch of a bank and – as she points out – she had been 'a success'. And yet she did not feel that she'd done as much as she could.

'I wanted to stop having to run around for other people. Do you understand?'

Actually, her loose hair, the hue of her lipstick, her tailor-made skirt, all tell me the same story as her narrative. When her father decided to retire, she bought up his company. She adopted a certain tone of voice when uttering these words, and allowed a short silence to follow them, like someone used to telling the same story who knows the points at which to create a certain effect. Then she repeats, syllable by syllable:

'Yes, I bought it up, from my own father.' That makes everything clear, and Barbara Netti likes things to be clear. Of
course, her 'own father' always comes three times a week,
and the manageress – 'who knows everything and everybody' – has kept the same people on the order book. When
she refers to these two, Barbara Netti pulls an affectionate
face – she wrinkles her nose, and raises her eyes heavenwards
– as if to evoke the good old memories of a period that was
admittedly dear to her, but which needs to be given a bit of
a shake-up. For six months, in her little company so white,
with her forty or so employees, Barbara Netti says that she
has felt at home.

'But we're here to talk about you, Madame Aubenas. Who
are you?'

My résumé is lying in front of her and, sometimes, she jots
a few things down in the margin. I keep obstinately trying to
read them, and as a result I lose the thread; I try to concen-
trate on the things I ought to be saying, while all I can think
of is the cats on the roof, in the pool of sunshine.

It's Barbara Netti who picks up the thread. 'Here, it's a
family atmosphere.' Sometimes, when she arrives in the
morning, she herself makes coffee for her employees. She
tells them: 'Come on, drink, it's on me.' Each of them has
a cup. 'We get on well.' Against everyone's advice, Barbara
Netti has set up a system for reimbursing the cleaning staff
for their travelling expenses. '14 centimes per mile.' Another
short silence, immaculately paced. 'It's a start, of course, I
don't want to endanger the business. In any case, here, all the

employees are on a permanent contract, thirty-five hours a week.'

In cleaning, employers don't like to hire anyone for over twenty hours per week. I've often heard people say so. 'Women are more affordable at twenty hours than at forty in cleaning. You mustn't pay them any more. Anyway, they can't manage it physically.' With wages, it's pretty much the same. For all the jobs associated with cleaning, a collective convention has fixed the hourly rate just above the minimum wage, ten centimes or so extra. Not many who put an official advert in through Pôle Emploi, a state organization, apply this measure. I've often asked the advisors why they didn't ensure the law was respected. At one training session – but I forget which – one woman advisor told me she couldn't do anything about it. Only the other day, a boss called her: 'I'm going by the minimum wage, I don't give a damn about your branch agreements. And do it the way I say, or I'll put my ad in somewhere else.' The advisor went to see her manager, who started to despair over the drop in job offers since the start of the recession and the problems with the ministry if the figures continued to slump. 'Don't start to discourage employers, act the way they ask you to, don't contradict them. The offers aren't made to suit your desires, but theirs.' Anyway, there are no checks on employers, only on employees.

Barbara Netti promises to contact me within a fortnight, 'even if the answer is negative. If it doesn't work, it might work in the future: we often hire people.'

*

When I told her I wanted to contact the maximum number of employers, Madame Astrid, from the private bureau, finally advised me – as always – to go to the Cleaning Fair. This takes place every year, at the Congress Centre in Caen. Here I find myself in front of the stand of a company with a dreadful reputation.

In the queue, the woman next to me is short, with her grey hair done into a bun, a shoulder bag hanging low down to her bare and very white knees, under a dark-coloured flared skirt. She stares at me. 'We've met.' I don't think so, but I don't trust my memory: I'm not very good with faces. She insists: 'We've already queued together.' I still don't reply. Anyway, in this circuit of job-seekers, the same people are forever bumping into each other.

'You were in the job train, a few months ago.'

It's true. Now I can remember the woman with her hair in a bun very clearly. We had hung around for ages on a quay, waiting for a convoy that was going round France proposing jobs. The operation was being piloted by the management of Pôle Emploi marketing, as announced by gaudy posters: '150 jobs available in Lower Normandy'. The train had stopped in Caen for the day. The logos on the sides of the carriages were more or less the same as in every display of this kind: the Carrefour hypermarkets, the army, the Orange phone company, the national police force, or a few companies offering 'personal services'.

The same coincidence had placed us side by side, and I had noticed her already because of her bare legs, even though it had been much colder then. We'd given our résumés to some guys who talked among themselves, we were photographed by *Ouest-France*, we'd believed in it all – at least I had, as I always do believe. I'd never heard anything more.

'Me neither,' says the woman with the bun.

She explains to me that 'it's all arranged in advance, in these deals, like in the cinema'. She found this out later through a brother-in-law who was highly placed in the police force. People are pre-selected by collective meetings at Pôle Emploi, then texted and told to turn up and finalize the job on the quay. You don't stand a chance when you come just for a poster, she says. In any case, Pôle Emploi don't like people to present themselves directly, without going through them: if by chance they were chosen, the recruitment would no longer count among the positive statistics for their agency.

All at once, we give each other a big hug, asking each other with sudden warmth what's become of us. It's the same story for both of us: everything and nothing has happened, we work all the time without really having a job, we earn money without really earning a living. She's just been turfed out of one business where she was starting to make a niche for herself. She blames herself: she's always late. Once she's settled down in front of the Internet, she doesn't see what time it is, especially when she's on a small ads site where she buys and sells second-hand clothes. She's even picked up a nearly-new bread-making machine.

'And how much do you make per month?' she asks, in a tone of fake detachment.

'250 euros on the ferry, fifty or so here and there, nearly 400 in just one place, L'Immaculée. But none of it's permanent.'

From her sigh, I guess that she must be floating around in the same waters.

She comes mainly to meet the employers. 'You don't get to see them often,' and she holds her hand out towards the sky to designate a terrible, living, incomprehensible mass, moving overhead, high above us, deciding our fates.

Out of the forty or so cleaning firms in the region, nine have taken stands. Various others have desisted at the last minute; quite a lot have kicked up a fuss, accusing Pôle Emploi of not having been selective enough, the year before, with the unemployed invited to come and look for jobs at the Fair. The woman with the bun gives me a hearty nudge. 'Look, there's Monsieur Nardon, one of the big cheeses in cleaning at Caen, my social advisor told me.' She daren't imagine she'll get a job; she's left her résumé here several times, but they never phone her back. She might get an interview, perhaps . . . 'It would be a big advantage in my file to prove how much effort I'm making.'

Monsieur Nardon is rather nondescript, neither handsome nor ugly, neither tall nor short, neither rich nor poor. You try to read something in his eyes, but you can't see anything in them, just a block of determination. He strides down the aisles of the Fair, as if he were walking through his own stables.

Monsieur Nardon has managed, with his firm grip, to create a company out of nothing. He is said to have an impossible personality, a mixture of generosity and sudden outbursts of temper.

We tag along after him. He's giving a talk at the Fair. 'You'll see: there's a heart of gold behind the façade,' says the lady with the bun.

Monsieur Nardon has picked up the microphone. 'Jesus! We're living at a time when it's difficult to trust anyone. You get all excited about someone and then, six months later, you feel let down. So I hire this girl, she's fantastic. I believe in her. Anyway, if this happens, she'll fall pregnant by the end of the year. It's a risk. Too bad, I take her. Anyway, I only hire people with a car these days. We've sometimes financed people who seemed very willing and highly motivated to get their driving licences. We wanted to give them a chance, the files had been drawn up by specialized organisations. One of the guys never took the test, the other left a fortnight after passing. I found this disgusting. I don't do this any more. Now, I feel that anyone who doesn't have their licence is just one more difficulty, and I won't take them. In any case, you can't travel by bus ten hours a week, it won't work. You'll give up yourselves. A job is an exchange. You need to stop sitting on your backsides and knuckle down to it.'

There must be a good thirty of us listening to him. He looks at us. He's seen so many people 'like us', women trembling, resigned, hardworking, impatient, condemned, ambitious – all this humanity hanging on his words and hoping for a sign. He picks up the microphone again.

'For some people, the least grain of sand is an obstacle. The people who clock in at the factory would never even think of not turning up. It ought to be the same here. People look for jobs out of spite. We haven't got past the mother telling her daughter, "If you don't work hard at school, you'll be a cleaner." Our business is like a windmill: people come when they want. We're going to need staff quickly. I'm looking. Can't find anyone.'

We rush to Monsieur Nardon's stand, trying to be among the first to register. I'm in such a hurry that I don't see that L'Immaculée also has a stand in the same aisle. A saleswomen nabs me. 'Hello, Madame Aubenas, what are you doing here? Looking for work?'

We both laugh, with a fake, hearty, lingering laugh.

'Anyway, you're dressed up to the nines, Madame Aubenas.'

We laugh even louder and longer.

'It was Pôle Emploi that told me to come,' I reply.

'But that's perfectly okay, Madame Aubenas, I'm not criticizing. Everyone needs to keep their backside covered. I'd do the same if I were in your shoes. Anyway, have a nice day.'

I wander off, feeling ill at ease. I'm looking for a woman trainer, the one who was at our first session, when we learned how to use a shampoolux. A few days ago, she called me to offer me training on alternate days.

'Where do you work?' she asked.

'Mainly at L'Immaculée.'

'I'll call Monsieur Mathieu to see if he agrees.'

When I bump into her at the Fair, she's already phoned Monsieur Mathieu. 'He thinks you're good, but he's not sure you really want to put everything you've got into the job. He'll see. In my opinion, there's hope. You'd get something stable, with a diploma at the end of it. It would be really great.'

I have to fill out a new set of forms. My mind goes blank for ages at the question, 'What's your "star quality"?' I automatically abandon any idea of referring to any professional competence. My mother brought me up with strict principles: she always thought cleaning was a man's job and carefully kept me away from any object that could be used in this activity. This was what the period dictated – the seventies, feminism. Eventually I write: 'hanging on'. This makes the trainer laugh.

On leaving the Fair, I bump into employees from Pôle Emploi trying to pinch the green plants, laughing like schoolkids. Philippe is waiting for me outside. We were supposed to be going to walk round the Fair, last Wednesday, my only evening off. On the ferry, we work six days out of seven. Then, on Sunday afternoon, he'd proposed that we go to a stunt rally at Mondeville, with lorries and motorbikes, I think. I turned both offers down. Too tired. He sulked a bit. Today we're going to give the Tractor its road safety test.

'You're treating me like a husband,' says Philippe, before we've even revved up the car. He too is well dressed today: it's the first time I've seen him in a tie, not a bad one either, his hair combed right back and fixed with some sort of gel:

now and again a damp, blond-grey strand sticks up. He's slipped his wolf's-head signet ring onto his finger.

I ask, 'Why do you say I treat you like a husband?'

'Every time we meet up, we do married couples' stuff.'

'Like what?'

'We go to the supermarket, we go to the garage.'

I burst out laughing uncontrollably. 'Is that what you mean by married couples' stuff?'

Philippe puts on his nice smile, and says roughly, 'Watch it, be polite.' We drive through the Mondeville shopping centre. It's quiet today, almost nobody in the car park. In his view, it's not worth going round the hypermarket, it's not the right time. We get a coffee at McDonald's, with a hamburger, a grilled-for-two. Philippe has finished his stint as a temp and hasn't found anything else. He's still got his car problem. It drives him mad, listening to everyone on TV going on about how bad cars are, pollution and the need to use public transport. It's one of the few occasions when I've heard him getting irritable. He keeps saying, 'Organic, organic, every-thing's got to be organic now, even clothes. Suits me, but how're we going to get work that way?' Today, for example, he was supposed to be driving his son to a friend's birthday party. He had to bust a gut for a fellow card-player to lend him his Peugeot. He'd spent all morning washing it, he'd added a sun visor ('A classy thing, no writing on it, just dark, see?') and hung a deodorant on the rear mirror, with a vanilla punch perfume.

'The other kid's father is in oysters. My son doesn't often

get invited to social circles like that, I wanted him to be proud. You should have seen their house, a footballer's villa, no kidding, a Premier League footballer at that. There's a swimming pool and a cinema inside.' The parents had paid for wrestlers, real wrestlers from off the TV, to entertain the kids. They were going to wrestle in the garden, but as it had rained, they did it in the garage. That's why he'd put the tie on.

'It looks good on you,' I say.

He'd chatted all afternoon with the children's mothers, in a room whose purpose he did not grasp. He was the only man; the women laughed as they asked him why he wasn't at work. He said he had his business and was his own boss. 'What in?' the women asked. At this point, Philippe loosens his tie and looks at me. 'I felt a right idiot, I didn't know what to say. Tell me frankly if I screwed up. Promise? Okay: I mentioned a pizza van. Not sausage and fries, right? I said pizzas.'

The Tractor fails its road safety test. The brakes have packed up.

18

The ZAC

On the banks of the Orne, near the old warehouses, a dozen vans are parked on the quays, all their headlights extinguished. The weather's nice, almost mild, there are figures sitting on tyres, and their cigarettes make red points that move around in the dark. I remember that someone had told me, one evening, on the way home from the ferry: 'The whores from town are up and about.' It's not yet 5 a.m., the floating cafés in the marina have just closed. There's a gentle breeze, as warm as a sleeper's breath. I've got lost on the way to yet another job.

I've picked up work as a temp, again thanks to Madame Fauveau. We hadn't met since our first conversations and, by the time she calls me, the features of her face are starting to fade in my memory, an increasingly blurred image behind a haze of good will. The new company is at Colombelles, one of the old working-class districts around Caen, now partly converted into a ZAC. The Tractor started without coughing and spluttering, and I snuggle into its now familiar smell of warm caramel. I mustn't be late, as I was at the lab where little Wounded Innocence kicked up such a fuss.

When people in cleaning talk about this quest for work, they all say the same thing. The worst thing is this first time, or rather all the first times: getting up in the still-sleeping town, driving through the night towards unknown places wondering where you're going to end up. It would be exaggerating to talk of fear; it's more like a nagging anxiety on top of the basic tiredness that you can't get over. You live on your nerves, and on the hope that you'll finally get somewhere, but the goal seems ever more distant.

I've got lost near the docks, as I now realize. I draw up near the vans to ask my way. Two of the women sitting on the tyres get up. They trip over empty bottles, and there's a noise of broken glass. The one crushes out her cigarette amid crackling shards. What do I want? Neither of them speaks French. They wave their arms around in surprise. I realize that I've forgotten to switch on my headlights.

In the deserted streets, I drive along, stopping at red lights and junctions. I daren't look at the time. Just as I was about to give up, the company building looms up ahead of me, after a roundabout.

I can barely make out the building as I go in. I dash through the entrance hall with its bay windows. It is filled with a dazzling light but completely empty, sitting there in the endless blue of a starless sky. I have been told to ask for Marguerite, the head of the team. In the cleaners' room, at the far end of a corridor, she's deep in conversation with a woman colleague.

'I tried to scour under a desk to get it clean, and I had a real shock.' The other woman nods without looking up, moving slowly to save her strength. Marguerite seems even livelier in comparison. She continues, her cheeks flushed, filled with animation: 'There were piles of dust underneath. I wasn't expecting this, and yet I clean it regularly. Can you imagine?' She's probably nearly forty, but there's something youthful about her, a freshness in her laughter, a way of looking you right in the eyes.

The third girl on the team has yet to arrive.

A particular sector has been assigned to each of us. Marguerite shows me the bit I have to do, while I pretend to know it all already, with the zeal of the new recruit who spouts impressive technical terms that she's only just learned. Yesterday evening, on the ferry, a team leader asked me to train a new cleaner. Then Mauricette told me, 'You've got the hang of it now.' On the way home, little Germain pulled my leg in the car: 'Hey, haven't you got a big head!' He's not entirely wrong. I feel a bit more confident. In the offices, the individual instructions are actually always the same: empty the bins ('careful, remember you make the bags last as long as possible'), keep an eye on the manager's desk, don't forget the chairs ('Florence, the chair in front of the table needs to be really straight'). My sector includes two floors and a cafeteria, peaceful and well cared-for, not too difficult to maintain, so long as you don't hang about.

From the wing where I'm working, I can see the sun rising on a moor covered in tall grass and weeds, with seagulls flying over it. The ZAC has been carved into this scrubland, with its roundabouts, car parks, warehouses, and modern buildings. It's all calm, absolutely calm, the silence is as vibrant as a piece of music, sometimes underpinned by the whistling of a gusting wind or the cry of the birds. I tell myself that here I might be able to do a good job, technically speaking of course. During another temping period, I'd accidentally come across my colleague's secret stash of treasures, carefully concealed under spray cans and cleaning cloths: a packet of chocolate biscuits that she'd started and a radio, no bigger than your fist, tuned into a pop music station. I'd wondered how she had the heart to listen while she worked. Now I can see why.

At the end of the shift, I meet up with the girls in the big hall behind the bay windows, around the company's coffee machine. In the places where I've worked, I've never seen any of them use the drinks or snacks machines. It's not that it's forbidden. It's unimaginable. We'd rather avoid them – perhaps anxious not to incur the suspicion that we're chilling out around them – , except on the ferry, where everyone stops to give them a hearty kick and a punch, trying to extract something – coins or chocolates – from their carcass. We never buy anything from them. Without it ever being said, we know that these machines are not for us; they belong to a world of work to which we have no access, the world in which you pick up your mobile when it rings and don't have to calculate how much time it will take to go to the toilets.

This time, my three colleagues are standing in front of

the machine, quite relaxed, amid the first employees who are
thronging into the hall. And, as if it were the most natural
thing in the world, they're choosing a coffee, clutching their
purses. Marguerite even treats herself to some biscuits as a
bonus and they carry off all these spoils of war to our room.
It seems a bit much for me to imitate them on the same day.
I merely follow them towards the room, dragging my trolley
along with me. Wherever I go, whatever the make of these
trolleys, I find them just as difficult to manoeuvre: they roll
along, stall, turn whichever way they want, they are stubborn
beasts that I never manage completely to tame. This time,
the trolley bumps along grumpily at my sides, spluttering out
little drops of soapy water in its wake.

'Look out, you're getting water everywhere,' says
Marguerite's voice next to me. She puts down her coffee,
sponges up around my trolley, and then straightens out. She
smiles. 'It's odd,' she says, 'I was watching you just now in the
hall. And I was thinking: Florence has got a really strange
way of holding her mop. She looks like she's fighting it.' If
I had any sense for repartee, I'd say, 'I'm a bit tired today,
tomorrow it'll be perfect.' I don't say anything. What I'm
mainly thinking is, 'I've always been terribly clumsy at cleaning, but I'd do anything at all to be able to stay here with
you.'

The third girl still has her back to me. She turns round. It's
Françoise, the team leader from the White Horse. I give her a
friendly welcome. Initially she seems a bit reserved – perhaps
she's surprised to see someone popping up from another

sphere of her life. Françoise is a nice girl; her cowboy smile, a little crooked, breaks out almost in spite of herself. Françoise has tooth-ache on top of it all.

She and Marguerite treat each other as equals, two good workers, punctual, getting through their tasks efficiently, prized by their employers. Sometimes, in the morning, they ask each other how many contracts they're going to be doing that day, and for which companies – they're like the two star pupils in a class trying to come first. When Marguerite got married, she picked potatoes and chicory. She started working as a cleaner more than fifteen years ago. She found it hard to begin with, getting up at 4.30 every morning. She was often ill. She doesn't beat about the bush to say that she likes the job. 'Some people are ashamed of it. Not me. I love it.' She's felt for a long time that, in everything, you need to make a few sacrifices.

When she talks about her job, she refers to 'my' places: she found them and negotiated terms and conditions herself, one by one, mixing together all sorts of private employers and cleaning firms.

'I thought companies didn't like us being employed at the same time by other firms,' I point out to her. 'Don't they all want us to be loyal to just them?'

'In that case I'll send them my bills to pay,' says Marguerite. She slips on a short little jacket, a black one, laced up in front by a ribbon belt. She looks for her bag and remembers she left it in the car. For a while, there'd been thefts in the premises, they'd never caught the culprit. To avoid any suspicions arising amongst us, Marguerite had established the rule that no object of value was ever to stay in the cleaners' room. With a smile and a wave she heads off to her car, striding swiftly on her strong legs. She doesn't tell me that she has to juggle her timetable to work for a diploma in cleaning. For her, this is a personal matter. It all happens in her head.

After two or three days, I feel that I've always worked here with her.

When I return home, the names of children, yelled out loud, echo down the stairs and the smell of burnt toast hangs in every corner of the building. It's time to be at school, and everyone's late. My mobile rings at just the moment I open my door. At first I think I can recognize Madame Fauveau's sorrowful voice. No, it's another company, Caen-Net, one of the most important in the field – they even give their employees protective clothing. I left my details with them a few days ago, at the Cleaning Fair. They're offering me a really plum job: a month as a temp in an apartment block, for three hours every morning, with the possibility of a permanent contract if everything goes well. I need to file my application today and no later.

In a block of administrative buildings on the edge of the ring road, the offices of Caen-Net resemble most of those that I've seen in the sector: rather basic, a little gloomy, with weary, overworked women interviewing other weary, overworked women. The former are patient, and they do the photocopying themselves. None of the places that has hired me ever looked so comfortable.

For the first time in months, I stop off in a café that I pass every day without the idea of actually sitting there ever coming into my head. I have a *grand crème* at an outside table; nice and quiet, though I can't stop my eyes running up and down the price list. I take out a book. A noisy gang of students come down the streets of the pedestrianized zone: they've been occupying the university all morning to protest against the reforms. They don't know if the exams will take place this year, because of the strike. From a distance I recognize two of them who work on the ferry. Little Germain, who's the same age, had skirmished with them. This was the only time he tried to fight. He hissed, white with anger: 'So do you think you're already top brass or something?'

The next day, Caen-Net call me back. 'We've settled the dates: you start in three days.' Theoretically, I still have just over a week with Marguerite and the others, in the ZAC. I should call them to tell them that I won't be completing my stint as a temp. And all of a sudden this strikes me as impossible, it's more than I can manage to give up those few mornings with them, this new sense of comradeship, the coffee machine, the first sunshine on the moor. Even if the other job is much more attractive, I'll say no without a second thought. An irrational no, an absurd no, an uncontrollable no, but a definite no all the same. I feel that I'm back where I was months earlier, when I decided to leave for Caen and look for work there. It had happened the same way, I was acting on impulse or almost. I repeat, 'No.' The voice on the phone sounds surprised: 'Are you sure you're not doing something silly? You agreed yesterday. It's a shame. You know, we don't get openings like this very often. Good luck.' Out of the eight companies I left my references with at the Fair, only two, Caen-Net and one other – the one that's absolutely awful – have offered me any work. Monsieur Nardon and Barbara Netti have already put me back on my feet. I realize that I've got no fall-back position.

Now, at the ZAC, I'm having a cup of coffee with the others. Sometimes, the girls buy their lunchtime snacks here too, the ham and cheese in triangles, served in damp white bread, plastic-wrapped. They say, 'It's convenient.' The third girl, the one who always walks slowly, a few steps behind us, sometimes adds, in a monotone: 'People eat like that in offices and banks.' I usually make big sandwiches for myself at home when I need to. That makes her laugh. 'My parents used to do that.'

The date of Françoise's birthday is getting near, and her preparations have become a morning news bulletin for us. Who's coming? What will there be to eat? Her husband has already given her a ring and a golden heart which she wears, with a blush, over her big lorry-driver-style pullovers. There's another present in the offing. Everyone tries to guess.

Marguerite, like me, is always a little anxious. 'Have you remembered to hoover up the dog's hairs in the end office? Did you close the windows because of the storm?' I like her to worry, it means I can reassure her. The list of things I mustn't forget is tucked away in my pocket, discreetly folded.

Today, a girl from another sector of the ZAC has fallen ill

and Monsieur Médard hasn't had time to contact anyone to replace her. We'll have to do her share of the work as well as our own. We need to work as a pair to go quicker, which adds an hour to our morning's shift, and we're not sure we'll get paid. Marguerite says, 'I'll designate myself. Who's going to volunteer to come with me?' I do.

Time is of the essence: Marguerite has to get away at nine o'clock on the dot to get to another workplace on the Mother-of-Pearl Coast. We rush along, and her coffee gets spilled. This always happens on the days when we're short of time, inevitably. When we reach the new floor with the offices still to be done, we're out of breath.

I'm a tad nervous about working closely together with Marguerite. It's stupid of me, I know, but I'm scared she'll unmask me. After all, she's noticed how clumsy I am, manoeuvring the mop and the trolley. Since then, I have the impression that she's sometimes gazing at me with a certain puzzlement.

She gets through the work quickly, with regular, confident gestures. I find it hard to keep up with her and I compensate by frantic overactivity. I rush around in every direction, the vacuum in one hand, the soaked cloths, dripping everywhere, in the other. The sun is already high in the sky, setting aglow the offices where the first employees are arriving. They scowl when they see the cleaning isn't finished yet. Some of them ostentatiously take their seats even though they can see we're still in the room, shifting objects about as if we'd put them in the wrong places. The vacuum cleaner is still doing its rounds when the manager appears. He has to shout louder and louder into his phone to make himself heard. Doors are slammed. Eyes full of disapproval follow us along the corridor.

'Quicker,' Marguerite hisses to me. She can't stop looking at her watch. There are still toilets that need to be done. I dash over to them. It's okay, 8.55 a.m., we've finished. We run to the cleaners' room to pack the equipment away. Through the shiny, gleaming hall we've just cleaned, Marguerite's slender figure hurries ahead of me, striding along. To catch up with her, I manoeuvre my trolley jerkily. The bucket filled with dirty water sways violently; I give it a push on the other side to steady it. In silence, I see it overturn slowly onto the gleaming floor. Still ahead of me, Marguerite is taking off her apron as she walks along, laughing, glad that we've managed to make it in time, her mind already elsewhere. All at once, she can't hear me behind her. She has a sudden presentiment. She turns round. I try to keep all expression out of my face, nothing, my gaze vacant – I feel that even the colour of my eyes would be too expressive. Marguerite pauses for a long while in front of the brown foam spreading in thick rivulets, so quickly, already practically at her feet. The hall has been turned into a stinking puddle, with a floor cloth floating on the surface. There is a moment of complete silence. Then Marguerite says: 'You wanted to go one better than me because I spilled my coffee, right? You were just jealous weren't you?' We laugh, or rather she laughs and I pretend to. I say, 'I'm sorry, it's my fault. Go on, you're in a hurry. I'll look after it.'

On my knees in the hall, surrounded by the employees now flooding in, I take an hour to mop it all up. I don't remember seeing Marguerite leave.

The following day, my heart is in my boots. I wait for some sign from her, a scolding, anything. Nothing comes. Just as we're leaving, it's Françoise who comes up to me and says, 'I need a word with you'.

'Go ahead.'

'No, not in front of the others, it's none of their business.'

We leave the building. Standing next to the door, Françoise lights up a cigarette and takes a somewhat solemn drag. It's the White Horse campsite. The two dragons have just sent to L'Immaculée the list of their recriminations. Among the twenty bungalows that we cleaned the previous week, seven need to be completely re-done: in the dragons' opinion, the work was completely slapdash. Of these seven, five are on *my* list. Number 6 in particular was dreadful: the microwave had been forgotten, there was a stain across a compartment in the fridge, and a piece of paper had been left under a bed. Monsieur Mathieu had been planning to phone me himself, but Françoise put him off the idea. She's happy to do it. 'I'm the team leader, you know. It's my job to do this kind of thing. If I can't do it, what use am I?' There's a new job scheduled for Saturday at the White Horse: I haven't been included on the list. Françoise takes a long drag on her cigarette, and exhales the smoke high into the air, her head tilted back. Of course, I mustn't take it amiss. It's not any kind of a punishment, just a practical question, nothing more than that. She'll keep me informed. Far from calming the situation, her soothing words seem, on the contrary, to reveal its full gravity.

I can't work out what attitude Françoise expects from me. I want to be as clear as she has been. 'If you think I'm letting the team down, I'll give my notice in. It's not a problem. I don't want to create any difficulties between you and the campsite or Monsieur Mathieu. Tell me frankly.'

Françoise chucks away her cigarette, and leans back against her car with her shoulders hunched. She narrows her eyes and gazes into the distance, at the undergrowth whipped by the wind. She looks more like a cowboy than ever. We both walk back towards the hall and she turns off towards the coffee machine, where the other two women are already waiting, purses at the ready. I don't feel up to following her. My work with them ends in two days. Marguerite has still made no mention of the bucket of dirty water from the day before.

Françoise turns round, I can see the little heart glittering round her neck. She says, 'Don't worry. Actually, have you found other jobs with other agencies?'

I lie. 'I'm waiting for answers.'

I know I've just slammed all the doors behind me.

19

Mimi

We gaze out at the sea with Luce, a blue sea, a blue sky; even the breeze is blue and motes of sunlight float through it. In winter, the declining light and the fogs made the barriers around the harbour station at Ouistreham seem opaque. Waiting for the ferry, we used to feel we were cut off from the world, hidden away on the end of a quayside, shut off, out of it all. Today, the dazzling summer sunshine makes the wire fence as transparent as net curtains at the window pane. The street now seems really close, just a breath away. Through the metal meshes, we can hear families going by eating ice creams, the children racing each other up and down on their bikes, and people taking an evening stroll towards the beach at Riva Bella.

This afternoon, girls from the ferry have gone to pick up shells from the rocks; they'll eat them later, when they get home. The days no longer seem completely swallowed up by the wake of the ferry. Some of the girls haven't come in to work, even though they're down on the schedule. Others, conversely, have come to clock in even though they aren't on the list. Sometimes, there are no more than a dozen of us embarking with our cloths, and the evening goes by in one mad rush, so we can finish on time. Jeff, the big boss, has roared that he'll be coming to sort things out. Nobody knows when.

At the entry to the harbour, the pink and white lighthouse looks as if it were made out of sugar. What if we rented a mobile home for the season, 110 euros per week, a bit further out towards the dunes? It would be like a holiday. And how about heading off to work somewhere else, far away from the 'sanis'? 'I'd like something with children,' says Héloïse. Or with the elderly. Or in a canteen. It's always the same disjointed dreams that unravel in conversations. Two of the men have given their notice in: one has set up a bookshop selling comics, the other is handing out leaflets. Some are playing football, wearing the company's uniform. It's summer on the quayside.

'You see,' says Luce, her eyes still fixed on the sea, 'if I'd worked less, I'm sure I'd still be with my partner. When I was in Paris, I did fourteen hours a day in a pork butcher's. And I have to say that the 2,000 euros were still there at the end of the month.' Luce has retired to Courseulles-sur-Mer. Her dog keeps her busy, and so does her garden. But the thing is, she's bored. She could get by doing nothing, it's not a question of money. She repeats this so often and so loud and clear that none of us can remain unaware of the fact. 'I can't do anything except work. So I found the ferry.' Luce doesn't hang out with the other pensioners, a small taciturn group of men and women near the little wall. Their pension isn't enough for them to live off. They'd all rather jump into the waters of the harbour rather than admit to this.

In the sunshine, even the car park seems less grey. Mimi gets out of her car, emitting waves of perfume and warm air. There's a very loud CD playing on her car stereo; it's the one she recorded specially to come to the ferry; it's mainly about three-masters and abandoned captains. When she makes certain movements, her pirate trousers and her white short-sleeved blouse give you a glimpse of her belly. The car door is still open, the music belting out. Everyone turns to gaze at her, instinctively. When Mimi appears on the scene, things never quite follow their usual course.

With a single glance, Mimi has weighed up who is here and who is not. She makes straight for a new recruit, a frail, nervy young man, and asks him in her somewhat husky voice, 'Have you got a couple of minutes? I've a few very personal questions I need to ask you.' Some girls have vaguely started to dance next to her car. We can no longer hear what Mimi is saying, but the new boy's ears are turning redder and redder, and he daren't look up.

Little Germain's eyes keep slipping across to Mimi: he can't help himself. In front of a group of riff-raff nudging each other, he adopts the voice of an important man: 'Weekends, I'm as busy as a cabinet minister. You can't ask me for any favours, I've got a mate to see every ten minutes. Evenings we all go to the disco together. When I get onto the dance floor, nothing'll drag me off it until five in the morning.' Little

Germain says that he's known in the Hammerhead Club in Le Havre, and even at Thorigny-sur-Vire, at the Lakeside Echo.

Near the harbour station, scumbags and old gals are quarrelling over the new uniform that's just been given out in the offices of the quai Carcot: black trousers and polo shirt instead of the striped overalls. It's a great event. Some of the women are swaggering: Jeff himself, they say, chose their outfits, estimating their sizes with a single glance. 'He's got eagle eyes – my husband wouldn't have weighed me up so well,' says one of the girls. Like a model on the catwalk, she pivots, sways her hips, and lifts the polo shirt to show off the tight fabric on her backside. Another girl films her on her mobile, shouting half-jokily, 'Swing your hair, swing your hair!' Mimi's music is still playing. Some women swear they'll never wear the new outfits: they look extremely annoyed, though nobody knows why. There's a silence. Everybody knows they'll have the uniforms on tomorrow, except perhaps Monique: nobody in Ouistreham can boast of ever seeing her in trousers; and the same goes for Stinkball too – though this doesn't matter.

In the distance, the ferry moves forward, its great mass haloed in a haze of water vapour and sunshine, my dear old ferry – the only job, no doubt, which I can still count on.

I'm in a team with Thérèse, who's also employed by the council and works shifts in a mini-market. The family get by: they grow their own vegetables and the husband works as a road mender. She's going to give me some professional advice on how to sort out the *sanis*. We set off. This sort of heat, which I'm starting to be very familiar with, gently rises into my chest. I soon feel as if smoke is going to come pouring out of my eyes and nostrils. But instead it stays burning inside me. I sometimes sense it smouldering away until it's time for me to go home. Thérèse goes three times as fast, and doesn't even seem to get warm. I stumble and fall over. She doesn't dare laugh. She says I'm not to worry, it took her ten years to get used to it. Near the cinemas, which show films all night, little Germain pushes his vacuum along, as seriously as a teenager. 'If they ask me to put the vacuum round, I'll do it properly, until the crack of dawn. I'm a warrior.'

Uniforms suddenly invade a gangway. Orders, shouts, laughter, all mingle together in the sour fumes from the spray cans. Everyone bumps into everyone else and treads on their toes. Then, once the cabins have been done, the corridor suddenly empties. We want to join the others but they've vanished. In one cabin, Sabine is conscientiously sluicing out a plastic cup left by the passengers, and filled with a blue, murky liquid with bits of cherries bobbing about in it. Everyone pulls her leg and she grumbles, 'I only drink out of the glasses where there's any alcohol.' There's a half-hearted rush for some leaflets singing the praises of an amusement park, found in a luxury class cabin. In one corner, one of the girls is French kissing a steward while all around the working girls slave away on all fours in the showers. There's a rumour going the rounds from cabin to cabin: it's one of Mauricette's good days.

I hear the new boy talking to Jordi, a shady character who boasts of having got up to no good – break-ins, mainly.

'D'you fancy her?' asks Jordi.

'Who?'

'The tall one over there, the one you were talking to on the quay.'

'Mimi?'

'That's her.'

'Who wouldn't fancy her? She's the prettiest.'

'Well, that girl's a guy, or at least she used to be a guy.'

The new boy has stopped dead in his tracks, as white as a sheet. 'A guy?'

'In Ouistreham, we've all known each other since we were kids at school. Mimi used to be a guy. I'm not lying. She works on the ferry so she can afford some more operations. She talks about herself – she's proud of it.'

The new boy just can't believe it. He shakes his head, stunned and incredulous. He explains that you can spot a transsexual a mile off. When his father ran a bar at La Grâce de Dieu, he knew one – a guy who was already old, dressed as a woman, but with a man's wrinkles. Everyone knew. Sometimes, to mock him, someone would tie him to a bus stop and the children would come and chuck stones at him.

'Ah no,' says Jordi. 'Mimi's the prettiest. That's all. That's all there is to be said.'

I seek out Mimi's long, elegant shape, with her basket of cloths hanging from her arm, a princess paying a visit to the *sanis*, making the heads of all the captains turn. The gangway is already empty. Even the two boys seem to have vanished into thin air. I feel I've been dreaming, but of what? Is the illusion the conversation that I've just overheard? Or is it Mimi?

Thérèse walks along with her mop, thinking over what she's going to serve up for lunch tomorrow. She's talking without really talking, the way people hum to themselves. 'And what about you, do you like roast pork, you know, with some little potatoes? Once I made a mince, but my husband finds it hard to digest.' I take her by the arm and even have to shake it without realizing. 'Thérèse, listen, is that true about Mimi?' She jumps, her thoughts still slaving over a hot stove. I must look so flabbergasted that she shrugs, raises her eyes to the sky, looking at me as if I were an innocent country mouse interrupting her train of thought over some trifle.

'Mimi? Yes and? What about Mimi?' says Thérèse.

Suddenly, I'm the one who feels embarrassed. 'It's not a problem. I just wanted to know.'

'Why do you have to kick up such a fuss about it?' says Thérèse. 'You're being silly. Everybody knows. For us, Mimi is just Mimi. We like her the way she is.'

In the car on the way home, little Germain can't stop babbling, as charming as a child. A few days ago he went for an interview in a pharmaceutical laboratory, with the possibility of a permanent job at the end of it. Yes, a permanent job, a real one. As a worker – that would be fine, little Germain says that's his level. A worker has a home, a wife, a wage. He still believes in it all, as much as ever.

*

I haven't been back to Pôle Emploi for a long time; it seems like it was in another life. The next day, here I am again. It's still the same crowded but silent space, imbued by a vague sense of awkwardness that hugely intensifies the least gesture.

Some advisors are talking about the restructuring of the agency – two of its branches have just merged. The advisors haven't been kept up to date, they don't understand what their new job is going to be. There are training programmes in the pipeline, but not enough. You sense they feel lost.

All the computers are occupied. I stand waiting, reading a brochure on the duties of a job-seeker. Now, I can't get a sort of irritating craving out of my head. I've got a sandwich in my pocket, but I daren't take it out because of the crumbs, and I don't want to go away in case I miss my turn on the computer. I finger my sandwich, I'm even hungrier, it almost makes my mouth water. I tell myself that everyone must have noticed.

At the reception, a woman job-seeker is waiting, looking annoyed (of course) but mutely so: her eyes are filled with reproach. You feel that she is choked with grievances that she daren't express, grievances that have been going round and round inside her for ages. She must be preoccupied all the time, especially at night, by the need to come to the agency. She has to come once a week, it takes up the whole day, she knows this, she has to come by bus from Dives for a twenty-minute interview at Pôle Emploi – and sometimes it's just twenty minutes, as it was last time. In an office that's open to the four winds, there's an advisor sighing all the more heavily because he won't have anything to offer her. And meanwhile, on every channel, she hears politicians explaining that the unemployment figures aren't as bad as all that. It's enough to drive you mad. She longs to be back in Dives; this now strikes her as the only thing of any importance: get back to her flat, her children, terra firma, as if the rest of the world was lacking in solidity. And after all, what does it matter if she is taken off the Pôle Emploi register?

Last time, she had been told to attend a special information meeting, with a group of people who had done the same job as her – accountancy. She'd simply had to wear a suit – you never know – and her mother, who had come to look after the children, had shrugged: 'The severance pay they give you won't even pay for the dry cleaner's.' On arrival, they'd been obliged to tell their life stories over yet again in front of the whole gathering, enumerating the fateful moments that had led each of them to unemployment. As if she didn't think about it quite enough already!

Then, nothing happened. It had transpired quite quickly that Pôle Emploi actually had no new announcements to make at this meeting.

Some of the people in the group had protested. There were some bitter jokes amid a general uproar. 'So basically, this is an information session without any information?' 'Why have we been made to come?' One advisor had eventually explained the 'instructions' that had been given to them, here and elsewhere, and for a good while already: the unemployment figures need to improve, whatever happens. This meeting was one way of doing this. You call a meeting for a category of job-seekers, executives, people on minimum welfare, it doesn't matter. Some won't come, and without any justification they become mere statistics. They'll be taken off the register. 'It's not serious,' the advisor had said, appeasingly. They can re-register later if they want, but this allows them to bring the figures down, even if only for a few days. The advisor, who had started to speak reluctantly, had poured it all out – the little schemes to massage the figures, the contracts for lower-cost associations, the phoney formulae for young people, or the aid given for part-time assistants which encourages employers to hire two half-timers rather than one on full-time. He said he regretted this, but it wasn't their fault. He wasn't out to con them; the whole system was at fault.

The woman from Dives is still waiting at the reception booth. Now it's her turn. She leans towards the advisor and it's already an enormous effort for her to ask him calmly: 'Why do we have to come for a meeting every month?'

'It's a government requirement: all job-seekers in France have to come to a meeting once a month.'

At first she doesn't reply. Then: 'And you have to interview us, too?'

'Yes. If we don't see people at the right time and place, an alarm goes off on our computers. We get punished too. No more bonuses – we lose our rating.'

Another silence: one so heavy that it suddenly seems the situation has become more serious. In certain agencies, every advisor sometimes has over 180 job-seekers on his or her files, when he ought to have 60. The region is over 4,000 files behind. Nobody can keep up any more.

The woman from Dives leans towards the man again and says, 'Bad luck. Chin up.'

At last, there's a computer free, the one whose printer doesn't work. The printer of the man next to me doesn't work either, but nobody has the heart to grumble. I can still feel my sandwich in my pocket, it's gently crumbling away. It obsesses me. There are four small ads that might suit me, one of which, in a hotel on the coast, has already been withdrawn by the time I phone. 'We're waiting to see how the reservations go. We're not even taking on any summer temping jobs this year,' the personnel office explains.

I find Philippe outside my place, in a tee-shirt with the slogan 'Welcome to the Sticks'. He's eating a special kebab, fries, and mayonnaise, and he's kept half for me. My sandwich has disintegrated totally in my pocket. I've completely lost my appetite, I feel rather sick, but I force myself to swallow some fries to please him. Philippe has come from Bayeux by train, specially to see me. He's very excited: 'Do you remember the oyster farmer's wife?'

I can't remember. I just don't understand but he simply gets even more carried away. 'Let's sit down, we'll be more comfortable.' We go into the shop where he bought his kebab, we order a couple of Cokes. With some paper napkins, he wipes the table and my chair before I sit down. I can see that he's trying to stay calm, but it's not easy for him.

'Yes, you know, I met that woman when I took my son to hers for a birthday.'

'And?'

'She's phoned me back. She's giving me a chance. That's not quite what she said, but I'm giving it you in a nutshell.'

'She's found some work for you? I'm really glad for you, Philippe.'

He gazes at me in perplexity.

'Do you really not get it, or are you just pretending? I don't want you to be sad.'

'Whatever for?'

'I'm having an affair with her. I won't be able to call you so often. You don't mind?'

20

The Permanent Job

There are six of us. We're dying for work. We're off to the White Horse campsite, of course. Françoise finally told me that, this time, I'd be on the next trip. Another chance. The phrase hasn't been uttered, but I can imagine I heard it.

The bad news – and Françoise seemed embarrassed, which doesn't happen very often – is that Madame Tourlaville isn't coming. She's gone for good. There are no more details about the reasons for her disappearance than we had on any of the previous ones. It comes as a shock to me; my voice must sound odd, since Françoise replies, more of a cowboy than ever: 'Anyway, *I'm* still here. That's the main thing, isn't it?' She's right, yet again. We're the only two left from the departure team. We look at one another: we pull a face and, at the same time, we laugh.

The four new recruits are in the courtyard of L'Immaculée, three women and a man, ready to embark in the van. Today each of us, one way or another, is staking his or her all. I've just come from the ZAC, where I laid into a staircase whose steps seemed a bit in need of attention. After, I had a cup of coffee with the others, at the coffee machine. In Françoise's hand, the plastic cup was trembling with feverish exhaustion. Every so often, she is overwhelmed by emotion, she seems completely to lose control. At other times, she appears lost in her own thoughts, silent, as if distraught. 'You're working too hard, you need to be careful,' Marguerite told her. Françoise grouched that it wasn't anything, maybe just the escalope she'd had the day before. Or a bug. She was okay, anyway. And she suddenly straightened up, to look stronger. Marguerite started to talk about her nephew's first communion and we all started thinking about other things. She still hasn't mentioned the bucket I spilled; she obviously doesn't know how to go about it. I sense an awkwardness between us. It was my last-but-one day with her.

Now, it's still not 8.30 a.m., the van has just set off for the White Horse, and Geneviève – whom I didn't know before slamming the car door a few moments ago – tells me all about the fifteen miles she does every day at dawn for two hours' cleaning ('It's awful, Florence, they're offices but there's as much mud there as you'd get on a building site. Anyway, I'm not complaining, that's how it is'). We talk about her husband ('Thank God, Florence, he's left'). Money, too. Geneviève has always heard people talking money, she's always seen them counting out coins, even the littlest coins; she only ever buys things she knows the exact price of. She says, 'Money – I think it's my first childhood memory.'

The road follows the line of the ploughed fields, with colourful service stations every so often, fringed with bunting like an open-air dance hall. The air is clear and transparent, it makes everything gleam, and this road, which I know by heart, looks new to me. Sometimes, the stream of cars is slowed down by a caravan which we eventually overtake, sounding our horn. Through the windows of the van, we get a whiff of holidays amid the gusts of heat.

When Monsieur Mathieu, of L'Immaculée, offered Geneviève a shift on a campsite, her response was positive. Completely positive. Positive, the way a jobs advisor tells you to be. She even waxed enthusiastic. She's going to prove to them that she's ready for anything. She's going to be a success.

On arrival at the campsite, I walk more stiffly, with movements that seem robotic, thanks to my anxieties. The two dragons barely spare us a glance – this is part of the ritual – and they start to list their reprimands for the previous week. Everyone takes on an air of contrition, apart from Françoise, who rarely resists a few grumpy protests. Then, reluctantly, as if we didn't deserve it, the dragons hand over the keys to the bungalows, their eyes already filled with next week's sermon. We mechanically turn on our heels, while Françoise, her head held high, picks up the bunches of keys.

In the cleaners' room, she tells us that she had a good long think yesterday evening at home, and so that we get a good idea of the activity she's referring to, she taps her forehead several times with her index finger. Françoise has also 'been told off' by L'Immaculée because of the way she manages the team: she needs to solve this permanent problem of people being late and not up to scratch with work. So from now on we're going to work in teams of two. Then, to motivate us more highly, we'll be paid per bungalow rather than per hour. There. The smell of detergent mingles with that of the recently mown lawn. We're paired off, in an atmosphere of general goodwill. We're all ready to start.

It's at this point that Monsieur Mathieu suddenly appears, as sleek as if he'd just emerged from his bath, slightly formal. With a little effort he could be smiling. Monsieur Mathieu has persuaded the mayor to renegotiate the contract with the White Horse which he himself had signed. It's all going to be sorted, he has high hopes of that. He rubs his hands, looks at the sky, and takes his sunglasses off. Yes – he's smiling! 'I'll make up the teams.'

Why on earth do I call out, 'We've just done it'?

Monsieur Mathieu swings round to me. He tries to contain his annoyance, but doesn't quite manage. 'Let me say it again: *I* am going to make up the teams. It's *me* that's going to do it.'

We'd have had a good laugh with Madame Tourlaville. I imagine I can see her, with her freckles and her eyes as round as a street urchin's, leaning towards my ear and murmuring, 'Not only are you going to shut it, but in addition you'd better hunch your shoulders and let your arms dangle in front of you to show him that you're really sorry you opened your big mouth.' So this is what I do.

Monsieur Mathieu puts his sunglasses back on and makes up the teams in a different order.

I've been paired with Roland, a cute little blond guy, who,

while sponging the table in bungalow no. 12, describes his 'vocation' to me in exalted tones. 'I love this job. I discovered it by chance a year ago, I can't manage without it.' A strong wind has suddenly risen: it makes the shutters bang to. A family try to fold up their deckchairs, struggling against the gusts of wind.

In the third bungalow, we start to get muddled in checking the saucepans and dividing out the sheets. In the fourth, we keep bumping into everything, like insects banging into a window. In the fifth, our heads spin, our arms flop. We still have three bungalows to go. It's started to rain – just a few drops to start with, so thin that we didn't notice straightaway. The washing we left outside is wet. We need to do the windows again. The work will never be finished by 1.30 p.m., or even by 2 p.m. One after another, the new recruits realize that their whole organization is collapsing. Some of them say they absolutely must go and get their children, but we're all stuck together: there's only one van. Their day, always unpredictable, a tightrope act, is turning into a disaster. So the atmosphere is one of a general stampede, with everyone phoning to warn the schools and their husbands, to find someone to look after the younger children or open the front door for the grown-up ones, and someone else to do the shopping. 'If I have to pay somebody to step in at the last minute to look after the kids, it'll take all my day's wages,' laments one young blonde.

Through the window, I can see one of the dragons going round on her bike. The door of our bungalow is flung open.

Monsieur Mathieu enters the room. 'How far have you got?' Without waiting for an answer, he jumps on Roland. 'How on earth do you think you're cleaning this table? Are you thinking of selling it or something? You don't do it like that!' He snatches the cloth from Roland's hands, folds it into four a few inches away from his face, as if he was going to give it a good wash. Then, moving like a gondolier, but more frenziedly, Monsieur Mathieu starts to rub the table himself, shouting, 'You need to do it in big energetic sweeps. Come on now, wake up for Chrissakes!' He goes out.

At 4 p.m., Monsieur Mathieu says to Françoise, 'With your new organization, you've made the work last even longer. Congratulations.' Françoise's face is glistening with sweat, she can hardly walk, her sturdy shoulders are sagging as if emptied of their flesh. Where does she get it from, the deep and firm voice in which she affirms, against all expectation, 'No problem, we'll get there'?

Roland swears he's not coming back, 'Never, never. It's an insult to our great profession.' Geneviève is haggard. She can't make any progress. She's shivering. She starts off another piece of work and keeps repeating, in a daze, 'How'm I going to manage? I need to eat. Where can I find something to eat?'

I have my last meeting with Madame Astrid, from the private bureau. In a few days, she's going to Portugal on holiday with a female friend. She shows me her arm, as round as that of the statues in the gardens of the villas along the race track.

'The only thing that worries me is the sun. Have you seen how white I am?'

In general, the private bureau manages to get jobs for half of the job-seekers sent to them by Pôle Emploi (Madame Astrid uses the term 'placing them', and I too feel it's the right expression). This year, she's not going to make her target of 50%. Too hard. Too deep a recession. I daren't ask her to specify whether I'll be in the lucky half or not.

She gives me one last piece of advice: I ought to aim a bit higher. Can I type on a computer, even a bit? She insists, 'Your file is one of the best ones I had. I'll continue to call you if I have anything for you.' She also suggests that I drop by whenever I want, to do some photocopying or to use the Internet. We shake hands and I go down the stairs.

When I go to check out the overall results of my time on the books of Pôle Emploi, the premises look empty. Some consultants have come from Paris to organize 'psychological help' for the agencies' staff. The advisors have been asked to attend, in the same way that they ask job-seekers to attend. They have to talk about their 'problems', each in turn, in front of everybody, just as they make others talk about theirs. The same thing has been explained to them as they explain to job-seekers: 'Learn to draw a line under the job that you used to have. You won't be able to influence the situation or act against the political plan: you may as well just let go. If you resist, you risk getting depressed. The days when things really aren't going well, take your car, drive round the ring road, go into a field, and yell.' Apparently, in 2013, after the presidential elections, Pôle Emploi itself might become the object of a social plan and start to lay off staff.

I have one day left at the ZAC. Everything else is vague, apart from the ferry. I spend the afternoon with Victoria. We drive through Caen, along the Orne. The sun beats down on the river, matt and grey, slate-coloured, lined with big square apartment blocks, built after the bombings. Victoria would like to show me one of the houses where they used to print out trade union leaflets in her day. We go past a row of new houses, beige and brown in colour, like the cream cakes that are sold in Intermarché in plastic containers. Part of the town's populace continued to live in shacks, long after the end of the forties, but today all that is left are the 'Swedish houses', houses in stone and wood, given at the Liberation by the Stockholm government. They are so robust and well planned that their inhabitants have never wanted to leave. We stop in front of a little villa in millstone. 'The tracts, I think it was here that they were printed,' says Victoria, uncertainly. A curtain twitches, shadowy faces hover at the window. Victoria can't remember. We leave.

At every street corner, we come across her story. She sleeps badly at night because of this past which constantly re-surfaces. To take her mind off it all, I want to show her the building where I work in the ZAC. When we get there, she is even paler. 'But this is the old site of the Normandy Metallurgical Society!' Where I could see only scrubland, there had extended hundreds of acres' worth of what Caen called the 'workers' fortress', barely a decade ago: a real little township of some thirty or so buildings, with blast furnaces producing a steel that, at the start of the twentieth century, would dethrone that of Le Creusot and La Sarre. The Normandy Metallurgical Society gave its noise and colour to the whole city, that red sky with the shadow of the five chimneys that could be seen on every photo, that permanent throbbing sound that the wind carried across every street, sometimes interrupted by the siren.

From the 1970s onwards, there was talk of crisis. From the 1990s, there was talk of closure. Nobody imagined it could be true. Even if the NMS was laying off workers in thousands, the unions continued to urge people to struggle, the management had just had the cafeterias revamped and the external painting redone. Victoria's husband worked there, he couldn't imagine any other form of life. When the factory finally did shut down, on 6 November 1993, he fell ill, that very same evening, seriously ill, like so many others.

The factory was demolished, piece by piece, brick by brick – all dynamited. The chimney of the coke oven was the first to fall, in February 1993, then the blast furnaces in 1994, the three chimneys 26 feet high, the rolling mill and the water tower, the coal tower, the lime oven, the central shop floor, hundreds of feet long, the scrap iron yard, the oxygen steelworks and the central steelworks, the continuous casting that had just been built and that was meant to save the factory. The slag heap was the last to be broken up, in February 1998. There's nothing left today, apart from two abandoned graffiti-covered buildings, and pieces of rail track gradually vanishing beneath the moss. The plain has become a plain again, crawling with life, buzzing with insects. Victoria climbs out of the car and gazes at the moorland, standing as stiffly as if a national anthem were being played.

In Caen, people don't talk much about the vanished factory: those who lived through its history avoid coming this way; they take a completely different route, or turn their heads to look in the other direction. Many of those who work in the new firms these days say they don't know about it. The ZAC, built on a tiny portion of the site, is – ten years later – one of the second-generation businesses. The first, based on electronics, has already started laying people off. Today, the hospital is the biggest employer in town.

Victoria has a headache. I feel sleepy. I know I mustn't sleep. Sylvia phones me: at the union elections on the ferry, she's been elected as staff delegate. She's been campaigning for weeks, she's won, she can't get over it. She's just come from her first duty period, when everyone could come and check that all the overtime has been properly paid.

I ask her, 'And?' Nobody came.

The following day, everybody is already at the ZAC when I get there at 5.15 a.m. We swap a few hurried jokes while we fill the containers with hot water. Françoise's husband has given her a birthday present. Even if we're scared of running a bit late, we can't hold back: we all shout, 'So – what is it?' Françoise turns pink, tugs at her blue pullover (which is too big for her), runs her hand through her short hair (still a bit flat after her shower), and says, 'A day at the beautician's'.

I let them go ahead of me, Marguerite with her jerky gait, then Françoise behind her, swaying her hips gently, dragging the trolley like a horse by its bridle, and the third, a few steps behind, as if in slow motion. I can't help thinking, 'What a pain it must be for them to have someone like me in the team, always knocking things over and overrunning the schedule.'

In my sector, I finish the stairs and scrub a few radiators. Exhaustion pulses in my temples. On one table, some cakes are lying around, left there by an employee. I can't help passing by several times, resisting each time the temptation to pounce on them. Have I thought of everything? The chairs neatly arranged, the bins emptied without changing the bags, one last look round the manager's office. The atmosphere must have been stifling here, yesterday, upstairs, all the shutters are lowered. In a few days, the heat has turned the moorland white.

The little team comes to the coffee machine, gathering little by little. Marguerite has managed to pass her certificate of professional aptitude. She hasn't told us about it. I found out by chance, seeing her photo in the newspaper at the ceremony when the diplomas were handed out. She was saying, 'It's given me confidence. I was a bit lacking in that department.'

At the coffee machine, she looks at me askance; I feel she'd like to talk to me, but doesn't know how. She must be looking for some way of really astonishing me, of saying she can't understand how someone like me was ever hired.

Perhaps she's even wondering what I'm doing here, who I am. She's surely hampered by scruples and tact, that's the kind of person she is. She holds her plastic cup, dreamily; I don't know whether she's going to launch into speech. I'd almost prefer her to be brutal, to treat me as a usurper, an incompetent fool. Let's get it over with. The lack of sleep is making me tetchy. I tell myself, 'If she hasn't uttered a word to me once she's finished her coffee, I'll speak to her.'

Suddenly, Marguerite takes me to one side. I'm ready to hear anything, excuses are already burning my lips, I just hope I don't cry. It must be the overwork.

Marguerite seems very calm. She tells me that the girl I'm replacing is leaving her job. 'We thought we'd put your name forward and support you for the post: it's a permanent one. We'd be glad to work with you.' The conditions are, for the sector, miraculous: a contract from 5.30 a.m. to 8 a.m., paid at the rate of the collective convention, 8.84 euros gross per hour.

Among the rules I'd established for myself, one was that I would bring this experiment to a halt as soon as I was offered a permanent job. I didn't want to block anybody else's chances of a real job. The Tractor is waiting for me in the car park. All the way home, it's to the Tractor that I talk, at length, in confidential tones, uttering words about everything and nothing, the words I didn't dare say to the others.

I'd just got its brakes sorted, and it'd finally got through its annual check-up.

*

In January 2010, I came back to Caen after the break, when the streets were white with snow. The Christmas decorations were still lighting up the façade of the town hall in green and purple. In my street, the hairdresser's boutique has been replaced by a piano school which offers to teach you to play in twenty-four hours without knowing how to read music.

I'm looking for Marguerite and Françoise. I've come to tell them that I've written this book. Next to the railway station, I've rented a soulless, odourless vehicle, a car that starts first time, the car of a journalist doing a report, like the ones I'm used to. At 8 a.m., I park at the ZAC to catch them at the end of their shift. The hoar frost crackles under my feet. I'm intimidated.

In the big shiny entrance hall, I recognize only one of the girls from the team. Françoise is poorly, Marguerite has been promoted to another job since gaining her diploma. Her replacement drags her feet about giving me her number. When I come back out, a clear chill has replaced the black, icy night air.

My day is spent watching the clock, as I wait to see Marguerite – if I can do so – on her evening site. I finally reach some empty offices. In the distance, upstairs, I can hear the trolleys clattering. I take the lift, I cross a corridor, I keep looking for her. I find her just when I am least expecting it.

It is a real reunion, with laughter and memories exchanged under the grey neon light of the corridor. I can't stop asking her for news, trying to delay for as long as possible the moment when this bubble of intimacy will burst.

Acknowledgements

Thanks are due:
to the people in Caen whose lives I shared;
to the people I love who waited for me;
to Olivier Cohen.